East Anglia & The Fens

East Anglia and the Fens

Text by Robin Whiteman
Photography by Rob Talbot

Weidenfeld & Nicolson

London

Text and photographs © Talbot-Whiteman 1996

The right of Robin Whiteman and Rob Talbot to be identified as authors of this work has been asserted by them in accordance with the Copyright, Designs and Patents Act 1988.

First published in Great Britain in 1996 by
George Weidenfeld & Nicolson Ltd
The Orion Publishing Group
Orion House
5 Upper St Martin's Lane
London WC2H 9EA

British Library Cataloguing-in-Publication Data
A catalogue record for this book is available from the British Library.

ISBN 0-297-83511-4

Copy-edited by Jonathan Hilton
Designed by Paul Cooper
Map by ML Design

ENDPAPERS: *Wicken Fen, near Soham;* see page 37.

HALF-TITLE PAGE: *Salhouse Broad.* Just over a mile downstream from Wroxham Broad (the 'Queen of the Broads') and on the opposite bank of the Bure to Hoveton Great Broad, Salhouse Broad derives its name from the Old English word for 'sallow', or 'willow-tree'. Although the shoreline of the broad has been severely eroded by wash from passing boats, work on stabilizing the banks has recently been undertaken. The long straggling village of Salhouse, with its thatched parish church standing in lonely isolation to the north-west, is the centre of a thriving reed and thatching industry. From the car park at the northern end of the village a footpath leads to the Salhouse staithe, popular not only with boating enthusiasts but also with swans, geese and ducks. Wroxham, the 'Capital of Broadland', became the main centre for boat-building and holiday-cruising in the Broads after the arrival of the railway in the 1880s. Today, with its crowded moorings and busy shopping centre, it seems more like a sea-side town than an inland village. 'Roys of Wroxham' claims to be 'the largest village store in the world'.

FRONTISPIECE: *Denver Windmill, near Downham Market.* Built in 1835, the six-storey tower mill at Denver has an ogee-shaped cap, more typical of Lincolnshire mills than of those in Norfolk, which tend to resemble an upturned clinker-built boat. Ceasing to operate by wind power in 1941, it continued to grind corn by diesel power until the death of the last miller, Thomas Harris, in 1969. Now restored, it retains much of the original equipment including a Blackstone oil engine. The buildings adjoining the mill include the engine shed and granary. Denver Sluice, a mile or so west of the mill, stands at a major junction of the Fenland network of artificial drainage and navigation channels. Linked to the tidal Great Ouse, the first sluice at Denver was erected in the seventeenth century by the Dutch drainage engineer, Cornelius Vermuyden, who was employed by the 4th Earl of Bedford and the 'Adventurers' to transform the watery wastes of the Fenlands into productive agricultural land.

CONTENTS

ACKNOWLEDGEMENTS

Robin Whiteman and Rob Talbot would particularly like to acknowledge the generous co-operation of English Heritage (Midlands Regional Office) and the two National Trust Regional Offices of East Anglia and East Midlands for allowing them to take photographs of their properties and sites featured in this book. Additional thanks go to Diana Lanham, manager of the National Trust Photographic Library. The photograph of Sandringham was taken by gracious permission of Her Majesty The Queen. They are also extremely grateful to: Lady Juliet de Chair, St Osyth's Priory; Nicholas Charrington, Layer Marney Tower; Norfolk Lavender Ltd, Caley Mill, Heacham; John Talbot (G4AYV) for facts gathered over the air waves; and Mike Softley for information on SS *Vina* at Brancaster. Our appreciation also extends to all those individuals and organizations too numerous to mention by name who, nevertheless, have made such a valuable contribution.

**Other books by Rob Talbot
and Robin Whiteman**

The Cotswolds
The English Lakes
Shakespeare's Avon
Cadfael Country
The Yorkshire Moors & Dales
The Heart of England
The West Country
Wessex
The Garden of England
English Landscapes

Photographs by Rob Talbot
Shakespeare Country
The Lakeland Poets
Cotswold Villages

Text by Robin Whiteman
The Cadfael Companion

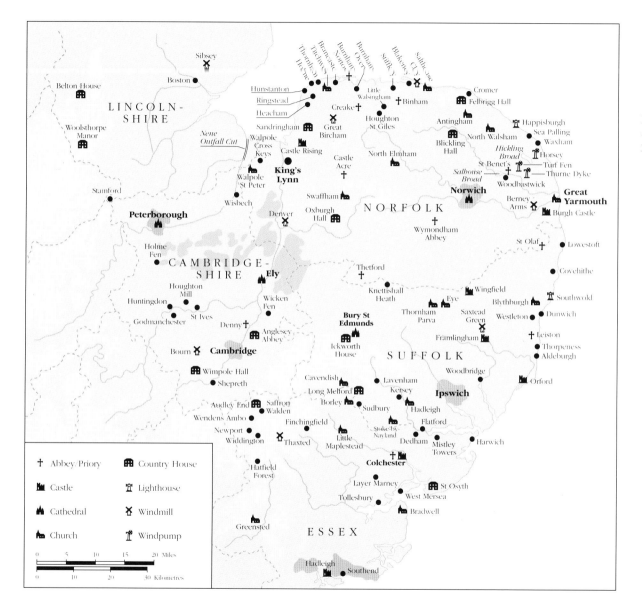

Map of East Anglia & The Fens showing the locations photographed for this book.

LINCOLN-SHIRE

Sibsey
Boston
Belton House
Woolsthorpe Manor

Hunstanton
Ringstead
Heacham
Sandringham
Walpole Cross Keys
Castle Rising
Walpole St Peter
King's Lynn
Wisbech
Stamford
Denver
Peterborough

Thornham Hale
Thornham Head
Brancaster
Brancaster Staithe
Burnham Norton
Burnham Overy
Stiffkey
Blakeney
Salthouse
Cley
Little Walsingham
Creake
Houghton St Giles
Great Bircham
Castle Acre
North Elmham
Swaffham
Oxburgh Hall

Cromer
Felbrigg Hall
Antingham
North Walsham
Blickling Hall
Happisburgh
Sea Palling
Waxham
Hickling Broad
Horsey
St Benet's
Salhouse Broad
Turf Fen
Thurne Dyke
Woodbastwick
Binham

Norwich
Berney Arms
Great Yarmouth
Burgh Castle
St Olaf
Lowestoft

NORFOLK
Wymondham Abbey

Covehithe

Holme Fen
CAMBRIDGE-SHIRE
Ely
Houghton Mill
Huntingdon
St Ives
Godmanchester
Denny
Anglesey Abbey
Bourn
Cambridge
Wicken Fen

Thetford
Knettishall Heath
Wingfield
Eye
Thornham Parva
Saxtead Green
Bury St Edmunds
Ickworth House

Blythburgh
Southwold
Westleton
Dunwich
Framlingham
Leiston
Thorpeness
Aldeburgh

SUFFOLK

Wimpole Hall
Shepreth
Cavendish
Long Melford
Borley
Sudbury
Audley End
Saffron Walden
Wendens Ambo
Newport
Widdington
Thaxted
Finchingfield
Little Maplestead
Hatfield Forest
Greensted

Lavenham
Kersey
Ipswich
Hadleigh
Flatford
Stoke-by-Nayland
Dedham
Mistley Towers
Harwich
Woodbridge
Orford

Colchester
Layer Marney
Tollesbury
St Osyth
West Mersea
Bradwell

ESSEX
Hadleigh
Southend

Nene Outfall Cut

Legend:
† Abbey/Priory
🏰 Castle
⛪ Cathedral
⛪ Church
🏛 Country House
🗼 Lighthouse
✕ Windmill
🗼 Windpump

0   5   10   15   20 Miles
0   10   20   50 Kilometres

INTRODUCTION

Poppyland,
near Cromer

After the railway reached the north Norfolk coast in 1877, Cromer began to attract increasing numbers of visitors. But it was not until Clement Scott's article in the *Daily Telegraph*, dated 30 August 1883, that the coastal area east of the resort, including Overstrand, Sidestrand and Trimingham, came to be celebrated for its wild and romantic beauty: 'It is difficult to convey an idea of the silence of the fields through which I passed,' Scott wrote, after a walk along the cliff-top, 'or the beauty of the prospect that surrounded me – a blue sky without a cloud across it; a sea sparkling under a haze of heat; wild flowers in profusion around me, poppies predominating everywhere.' 'Poppyland', as it came to be called, caught the imagination of the Victorians, brought inspiration to numerous writers and poets, and encouraged so many wealthy people to buy property in the area that Overstrand was dubbed the 'Village of Millionaires'. Today Poppyland survives more in the imagination than in reality. For those who remember, it was Scott's red-poppied 'Garden of Sleep'.

With its intricate network of rivers and drainage channels, stretches of coastal marshland and wetland expanses of fens and broads, East Anglia is dominated by water and, since much of the land is level and low-lying, the reflection within the water is invariably of a vast, uninterrupted and fluid sky. In *Hereward the Wake* Charles Kingsley summed up the uniqueness of the 'wild, wet, and unwholesome marshes' that once stretched from Cambridge to The Wash:

> 'Overhead the arch of heaven spread more ample than elsewhere, as over the open sea; and that vastness gave, and still gives, such cloudlands, such sunrises, such sunsets, as can be seen nowhere else within these isles.'

The cold northerly winds that bring a diamond-like clarity to the air, can also bring terror and devastation. When the wind blows hard from the north-west and the tides are at their highest, enormous quantities of water – funnelled towards the Strait of Dover – can build up into what is known as the North Sea surge. For centuries, many towns and villages around the east coast have fought a constant battle against storm, tide and flood. In some places the destructive power of the sea has proved too strong and large portions of the coast have been lost forever. Dunwich, once the seat of an Anglo-Saxon bishopric and a major medieval port, has now virtually disappeared beneath the waves.

Perhaps the most memorable flood of recent times was that of January 1953, when the lethal combination of a high spring tide and gale-force onshore winds caused a great tidal wave to burst through coastal defences and sweep inland, engulfing much of the low-lying area between the Humber and the Thames: hundreds of lives were lost, thousands of people evacuated and countless properties flooded or destroyed. The loss of much of the East Anglian coastline is not entirely due to horrendous and unpredictable storms, though the damage they cause is all too sudden and dramatic. Erosion, albeit gradual, causes cliffs to crumble, beaches to disappear and sand to be carried away. But while some parts of the coast are being consumed by the waves, others are advancing seawards due to silting and the movement of sand and shingle. In north Norfolk, for example, medieval seaports, such as Wiveton, Blakeney and Cley, which once handled ships of more than 100 tons, have either been marooned inland or their estuaries have so silted up that only small boats can reach the quays. Land reclamation through artificial drainage and embankments has transformed vast tracts of marshy wilderness, notably in the Fens, into valuable farmland, making East Anglia one of the richest agricultural regions in the United Kingdom. Indeed, it was as a direct result of the pioneering efforts of two Norfolk landowners – 'Coke of Holkham' and 'Turnip Townshend' of Raynham – that dramatic improvements were made in food production during the Agricultural Revolution of the eighteenth century.

In prehistoric times East Anglia was very much isolated from the rest of the country by malarial wetlands in the east and dense forest in the south. Although many of the trees have now been cleared, tracts of ancient woodland survive in the forests of Epping and Hatfield. The draining of the Fens in the seventeenth and eighteenth centuries not only converted marshy fields and stretches of water into productive farmland, it also improved and expanded navigation along the inland waterway network, thereby increasing trade between the Midlands, the Fenlands and the North Sea.

Despite the marked increase in commercial activity brought about by improvements in water and road transport, however, the region remained comparatively isolated until well into the second half of the twentieth century. It is not surprising, therefore, that many old customs and traditions were kept alive almost to the present day, especially a belief in witchcraft. Indeed, partly because of Puritanism, which the East Anglians embraced with zeal, and partly because of the anti-witch campaign carried out by such men as Matthew Hopkins – the self-styled 'Witchfinder General' – East Anglia found itself in the terrifying grip of witch-hunting hysteria during the seventeenth century.

For this book, East Anglia has been defined as the region of eastern England between the Thames estuary in the south and The Wash in the north, encompassing the counties of Norfolk, Suffolk, Essex and Cambridgeshire (which, since boundary changes in 1974, includes Huntingdonshire and Peterborough). The southern part of Lincolnshire has also been included because it embraces part of the Fens. Within this once-remote and once-highly populated region of England the landscape is essentially flat, but the flatness is deceiving. It is certainly not a land of drab and boring nothingness.

There may be no spectacular lines of mountains, rushing torrents and high waterfalls. There may be no startling surprises in the geology, apart from perhaps the coloured chalk cliffs to be found at Hunstanton. Yet the scenery – for all its far horizons – has an indefinable enchantment, an enchantment that produces mingled emotions of melancholy and joy (probably because of the inescapable presence of boundless expanses of sky). So, what need is there then for high hills, when the clouds can create mountains higher and grander than the Himalayas?

Through his methodical studies of cloud formations, John Constable clearly demonstrated that skies – often stormy – were the 'key note', the 'standard of scale' and the 'organ of sentiment' in his landscape paintings. The distinctive scenery of East Anglia (which is only partly represented by the old mills, green meadows and tree-shadowed waterways of the lower Stour valley where Constable was born) has been the inspiration for numerous artists, writers, musicians and poets: Thomas Gainsborough (1727-88), John Crome (1768-1821), George Borrow (1803-81), Charles Dickens (1812-70), Ruth Rendell (b. 1930), M.R. James (1862-1936), Benjamin Britten (1913-76) and George Crabbe (1754-1832), to name but a few. The ranks of the talented and famous (together with those who have had a major role in shaping the nation's history) are further swelled by those who studied at Cambridge, England's second oldest university town: Thomas Cranmer (1489-1556), Oliver Cromwell (1599-1658), John Milton (1608-74), Samuel Pepys (1633-1703), Isaac Newton (1642-1727), Charles Kingsley (1819-75) and Rupert Brooke (1887-1915). The birth of seamen such as Horatio Nelson at Burnham Thorpe in 1758 and George Vancouver at King's Lynn in 1757 confirms the truth of the old saying that 'a Norfolk man is born with one foot on the land, and the other in the water'.

The region's close proximity to the Low Countries and Germany brought great trade and wealth, particularly between the thirteenth and seventeenth centuries when large flocks of sheep grazed the 'brecks' and heaths, and the wool and cloth industry was at its height. As East Anglia had no fast-running rivers or coal, it mercifully escaped the negative effects of the Industrial Revolution. Today, the landscape is comparatively unspoiled. In addition to its remarkable number of churches – many of which were built on 'the backs of sheep' – the most characteristic feature of the countryside is the windmill; once common, but now, alas, all too rare. Some were used for grinding corn, while others were designed to drain the marshes.

As a boy, Constable explored all that lay on the banks of the Stour, including his father's mill at Flatford (powered by water, rather than wind). 'These scenes made me a painter,' he wrote in 1821, 'and I am grateful.' The mill is still there. So are many of the other places that he loved so well. Yet 'Constable Country' is only a small part of the East Anglian landscape. Its exploration invariably leads to water, and from water the eyes are lifted, almost in celebration, to the sky above.

But beware. If the clouds are blackening and the wind is gusting from the north-west, hurry to high ground. For the sea might just decide to return.

CAMBRIDGE AND SOUTH-WEST CAMBRIDGESHIRE

Houghton Mill,
near Huntingdon

Standing on a tributary of the
Great Ouse, the watermill at
Houghton dates from the seventeenth century and is one of the
last to survive along the river.
Much altered in the following
two centuries, the five-storey
brick-and-timber building, with
tarred weather-boarding and
slate roof (originally thatched),
had three large waterwheels and
ten pairs of millstones. The
waterwheels were removed in
1930 and replaced by sluices.
Now owned by the National
Trust, the mill – its partly
restored machinery powered by
electricity – continues to grind
corn into flour. Before the
Reformation, the mill belonged
to Ramsey Abbey, who forced its
tenants to grind their corn at
Houghton under penalty of a
heavy fine. Tension between the
villagers and the monks came to
a head in 1500 when the abbot
partially blocked the course of
the river and caused extensive
flooding of the surrounding
fields. The dispute, which
dragged on for 15 years, was
finally resolved by the King's
Court in favour of the villagers.

Situated on dry firm ground at the southern edge of the level peat-lands of the Fens and in the shadow of the gentle chalk slopes of the Gog Magog Hills, the university city of Cambridge originated at a crossing-point of the River Cam (or Granta) some 2,000 years ago. After the Claudian invasion of AD 43, the Romans established a small fort on the chalk ridge (Castle Hill) overlooking the river, from which a small Romano-British town (*Duroliponte*) developed. In addition to constructing the Car Dyke, a canal linking the Cam with the Ouse, thereby increasing the settlement's importance as an inland sea-port, the Romans built a bridge to carry the road from Colchester to Godmanchester over the river at *Duroliponte*. This road, one of four Roman roads to converge on the town, was given the Latin name *Via Devana* in the eighteenth century.

After the withdrawal of the legions at the beginning of the fifth century, the history of *Duroliponte* (meaning 'the walled town in a marshy place') is obscure. At some time during the so-called Dark Ages, the settlement was renamed *Grantacaestir* ('the Roman camp on the River Granta') and, by the end of the eighth century, it was a thriving Anglo-Saxon market town centred on the opposite, eastern side of the river to Castle Hill. Instead of developing into Grantchester (the name that was adopted by the village of *Granteseta*, meaning 'settlers on the Granta', two miles upstream), *Grantacaestir* became *Grontabricc* (the bridge over the Granta), then *Cantabrige* and, finally, Cambridge.

In 871 the town was sacked by the Danes and subsequently became an Anglo-Danish settlement. The Danish conquest of England, under Guthrum, was stemmed by Alfred the Great, King of Wessex, at the battle of Ethandun in 878. Guthrum, whose army was decisively defeated, was forced to sign the Treaty of Wedmore, by which he agreed to be baptized a Christian, to leave Wessex in peace and to remain in the territory east of Watling Street (later known as the Danelaw). Under his baptismal name of Athelstan, Guthrum was recognized as King of East Anglia and, in consequence, the region became subject to Danish rather than Anglo-Saxon laws and customs. A fairly positive indicator of settlements established during Danish rule are places with the suffix *-by* (meaning village). A heavy concentration, for example, can be found in the area north-west of Great Yarmouth, which includes Hemsby, Rollesby, Filby and Stokesby. Places with the suffix *-thorpe* indicate a secondary Danish settlement.

By the tenth century Cambridge was, once again, a busy inland seaport, trading – via the Cam, Ouse and Wash – not only with continental Europe, but also with Ireland. In addition to a mint, market and courthouse, the town – straddling both sides of the river – boasted at least five churches, of which only the late Anglo-Saxon tower of St Benet's survives. The conquering Normans secured their control over the river, bridge and town by erecting a castle on the site of the Roman fort, which, according to the Domesday Book, also involved the demolition of twenty-seven houses. Perhaps the most notable ecclesiastical building to survive from the Norman period is the 'Round Church' of the Holy Sepulchre, built in about 1130. From 1092, when an Augustinian priory was established near the castle (moving to a new site at Barnwell in 1112), numerous religious houses were founded in and outside the town. Exactly how and when the University arose in Cambridge remains unresolved, but tradition maintains that its origin stems back to the migration of teachers and scholars from Oxford in 1209. Thereafter, education ceased to be confined to the schools attached to the monasteries and, rather than living in accommodation provided by the monks or the townspeople, students gradually began to gather together in hostels. Two of the hostels were eventually combined to form the first of the residential colleges, Peterhouse, founded in 1284. Under the terms of the will of Hugh de Balsham, Bishop of Ely, the college was to be a secular foundation organized and administered in the same way as Merton College in Oxford (in other words, as a self-governing institution in which male students and teachers all lived together as a community). The first women's college (at Girton, some two miles north of the city) was not founded until 1869, however, and it was not until as late as 1948 that women finally achieved equal university status with men.

Today, in addition to being the home of Britain's second oldest university and an internationally renowned seat of learning, Cambridge is the county town of Cambridgeshire (enlarged in 1974 to include Huntingdonshire and Peterborough), and a leading centre of the high-technology revolution. Yet, for all its architectural wealth and commercial importance, the city's greatest contribution to the modern world has been in the thoughts and writings of the people who have studied at the university: Isaac Newton (1642-1727), Samuel Pepys (1633-1703), Oliver Cromwell (1599-1658), Lord Tennyson (1809-92) and William Wordsworth (1770-1850), to name but a few. One after another – like the motley procession of punts that makes the often erratic journey up the Granta, under the 'Bridge of Sighs' and through the 'Backs' of the riverside colleges – those who have 'come up' to Cambridge have found it to be a place apart: a city where dreams and aspirations may very well come true.

The Cromwell Museum,
Huntingdon

Oliver Cromwell, the soldier and statesman who ruled Great Britain as Lord Protector from 1653 to 1658, was born at Huntingdon on 25 April 1599. The house stood on the site of an Augustinian friary, granted to the Cromwell family after the Dissolution. It was almost entirely demolished and replaced by the present 'Cromwell House' in *c.* 1830. The Cromwell Museum – located further south along the High Street, opposite All Saints Church on Market Hill – was established in 1962. Restored to its present form in 1878, the museum building was originally the western end of the Infirmary Hall of the monastic Hospital of St John the Baptist, founded in *c.* 1160. Its conversion into a grammar school in 1565 included the insertion of an upper floor and the encasement of the stone exterior in red brick. Pupils at the school included Cromwell and the diarist Samuel Pepys. During medieval times the town had 16 churches. The much-altered All Saints church (left of photograph) is one of only two to survive.

Bridge and Chapel,
St Ives

Originating as the Anglo-Saxon settlement of 'Slepe' (meaning 'mud'), the old market town and inland port of St Ives stands on the north bank of the River Great Ouse, four miles east of Huntingdon. St Ives, the medieval name of the town, is derived from St Ivo, a Persian bishop, whose remains were supposedly found about half a mile east of Slepe in *c.* 1000. The abbot of Ramsey built a Benedictine priory on the site, which, by attracting pilgrims and traders, led to the development of a thriving market town. The earliest reference to a possible bridge over the Ouse at St Ives occurs in a Ramsey Abbey document of 1107. The present six-arched stone bridge, dating from the early fifteenth century, supports a rare bridge-chapel in the middle of the downstream side. After the dissolution of the priory in 1539, the prior – who seems to have been the only monk in residence at the time – was not only granted a pension of twelve pounds a year, but was allowed to live in the bridge-chapel for life.

Wimpole Hall

Set in 350 acres of landscaped parkland, Wimpole Hall is the largest and most impressive country mansion in Cambridgeshire. The central core of the house – seven bays across – dates from the period 1640 to 1670. Further alterations in the following century included: the addition of side wings by James Gibbs (one containing a chapel painted by James Thornhill, the other a library); the refacing of the north and south fronts in red brick to create a homogeneous style by Henry Flitcroft; and the creation of the Yellow Drawing Room and Bath House, both by John Soane. Much of Henry Edward Kendall's extensions in the 1840s, however, were later demolished by Mrs Elsie Bambridge, daughter of Rudyard Kipling, who bought the neglected and almost empty property in 1938. The park was laid out by such notable landscape gardeners as Charles Bridgeman, 'Capability' Brown and Humphry Repton. The ruined folly tower, based on designs by Sanderson Miller, was erected in 1774. Wimpole Home Farm, designed and built by Soane as a model farm in 1794, is now the largest rare breeds centre in East Anglia.

The Chinese Bridge,
Godmanchester

On the south bank of the River Great Ouse, opposite Huntingdon, Godmanchester has a history dating back to prehistoric times. During the Roman period the town, which was preceded by a fort, grew up at an important crossing point of the river, where Ermine Street was joined by roads from Cambridge and Sandy (east of Bedford). The Anglo-Saxon town, which retained the Roman pentagonal street pattern, became a Danish burgh in the ninth century, and eventually passed to the English Crown. In King John's charter of 1212, Godmanchester was made a self-governing manor of the 'ancient demesne of the Crown', only attaining the status of a free borough in 1604. The town is linked to Huntingdon by a medieval stone bridge across the Ouse. The wooden 'Chinese Bridge', at the northern end of the Mill Pond (close to the nineteenth-century Town Hall, which is now the Senior Citizens' Club), was originally built in 1827 by the architect J Gallier. It was rebuilt in 1869, replaced with a replica in 1960 and restored in 1979.

King's & Clare Colleges,
Cambridge

Cambridge was a thriving market Fenland town and busy inland port long before it became the home of the second oldest University in Britain. Its origins date back at least to Roman times, when there was a small settlement with a bridge over the Cam (or Granta). After the Norman Conquest, the town was dominated by a huge fortress on what is now Castle Hill. Traditionally, the university is said to owe its beginnings to a disturbance at Oxford in 1209, which caused many teachers and scholars to migrate to Cambridge. The first residential college, Peterhouse, was founded in 1284 by Hugh de Balsham, Bishop of Ely. Clare College (left in the photograph) was first founded in 1326 as University Hall. It was rebuilt between 1638 and 1719. King's College Chapel (centre) was begun in 1446 and completed in 1515. The Gibbs' Building (right) is named after its architect and dates from 1724. The riverside lawns and gardens, running parallel to King's Parade behind King's, Clare and other colleges, are known as the 'Backs'.

Bourn Windmill

Although the open trestle post mill at Bourn, built before 1636, is said to be the oldest windmill in England, it does not receive a mention in the *Guinness Book of Records*. In fact, the book states that the oldest remains of a windmill in the country is the fourteenth-century 'stump, wrongly known as "The Beacon", at Burton Dassett, Warwickshire'. Nevertheless, despite the absence of a precise date, the weather-boarded mill at Bourn is generally considered to be the oldest still surviving. This is because its design – unlike Pitstone mill in Buckinghamshire, dated 1627, and owned by the National Trust – most resembles the representations of windmills found in early carvings and manuscripts (in other words, having a steeply pitched and flat-sided roof). Owned by the Cambridge Preservation Society, the mill stands amidst gentle rolling farmland, near the village of Caxton, a mile or so north-west of Bourn. The tiled floor of the thirteenth-century tower of St Helen and St Mary at Bourn is decorated with a maze, rarely found in English churches.

'Willow Cottage', *Shepreth*

Eight miles south-west of the centre of Cambridge, the village of Shepreth – with its thatched cottages, manors and church (the latter dating from the twelfth century) – lies on the south side of the Cam (or Rhee) valley. Its name is derived from the Old English for 'sheep-brook', suggesting that the village stream may have been used for sheep dipping. Indeed, as John Layer, the local squire, rector and historian observed in the seventeenth century, Shepreth was 'environed on all sides except the south-east with rivers and brooks, and has a pleasant sweet brook besides running through the town'. Although there was a settlement at Shepreth in Anglo-Saxon times, evidence of Neolithic occupation has also been unearthed in the area. During the Middle Ages, the Benedictine nunnery at Chatteris, north-west of Ely, owned a small manor at Shepreth, the sparse remains of which can be found in Manor Farm. Docwra's Manor, near the war memorial, dates from the sixteenth century, but was extensively rebuilt in the 1740s. Its gardens are regularly open to the public.

ELY AND THE FENS

Standing on the site of a double monastery founded for both men and women in the seventh century by Etheldreda, Queen of Northumbria and daughter of Anna, King of the East Angles, the Romanesque cathedral at Ely dominates the flat fenland landscape for miles around. The Anglo-Saxon monastery was destroyed by the Danes in 869 and refounded as a Benedictine abbey in 970. The present church, which became a cathedral in 1109, was built between 1083 and 1189, and extended in the thirteenth century. In 1322 the Norman central tower collapsed, destroying parts of the choir, nave and transepts. It was replaced by a unique Octagon, supported by eight stone columns and crowned by a timber lantern, the whole structure weighing some 400 tons. Seeming to hang in space, it is an incredible feat of construction and an architectural gem. The Lady Chapel, completed in 1349, is the largest chapel of its kind to be attached to an English cathedral.

Before the Fens were drained in the seventeenth and eighteenth centuries, the city of Ely stood on the eastern side of a seven-mile-long, four-mile-wide island, surrounded by treacherous marshland. Even today, despite the systematic transformation of watery wasteland into rich agricultural farmland, Ely's Romanesque cathedral dominates the flat, almost treeless landscape for miles around. Indeed, the magnificent religious building, viewed from afar, has often been likened to a huge ship riding at anchor in a calm and oft-times misty sea. In the open-skied wide-horizoned immensity of the Fens, even distances can be deceiving, as Celia Fiennes observed when approaching Ely from Bury St Edmunds in 1698:

'Ely Minster is in one's view at a mile distant you would think, but go it is a long four miles.'

Daniel Defoe, in *A Tour Thro' the Whole Island of Great Britain*, first published in 1724-6, observed that fogs generally covered the undrained Fens in the latter part of the year:

'. . . so that when the Downs and higher grounds of the adjacent country were gilded by the beams of the sun, the Isle of Ely looked as if wrapped up in blankets, and nothing to be seen, but now and then, the lanthorn or cupola of Ely Minster.'

In the past, like many of the settlements that stood on ground slightly higher than the encircling Fens, Ely was one of the most isolated and least accessible places in England, reached either by secret paths or, when rising water-levels made them impassable, by boat. Although there was a super-abundance of fish and wildfowl in the fenlands, the damp climate was unhealthy, especially for outsiders. Yet, as Defoe remarked:

'. . . the people, especially those that are used to it, live unconcerned, and as healthy as other folks, except now and then an ague, which they make light of, and there are very great numbers of very ancient people among them.'

In the East Anglian coastal marshes of Essex, however, Defoe noted that there was a noticeable lack of women, and that the men frequently 'had had from five or six, to four-teen or fifteen wives; nay and some more'. One Canvey Island farmer, he was informed, was living with his twenty-fifth wife; while his son, in his mid-thirties, 'had already had about fourteen'. The reason, so 'a merry fellow' told him, was that the men were bred in the marshes and 'seasoned to the place', while their wives came from the 'uplands' out-side. It seemed:

> '. . . that when they took the young lasses out of the wholesome and fresh air, they were healthy, fresh and clear, and well; but when they came out of their native air into the marshes among the fogs and damps, there they presently changed their complexion, got an ague or two, and seldom held it above half a year, or a year at most; and then, said he, we go up to the uplands again, and fetch another; so that marrying of wives was reckoned a kind of good farm to them.'

The Fens, covering some 1,500 square miles of Cambridgeshire, Lincolnshire and Norfolk, have two distinct parts: the silt-lands (formed from sea- and river-borne mat-erial) around and bordering The Wash; and the peat-lands, or 'Black Fens' (composed of decaying vegetation), which lie further inland. The islands of firm ground that stood out above the surrounding low-lying marshlands were settled during prehistoric times. At Flag Fen, near Peterborough, for example, excavations have revealed the remains of a large Bronze Age timber platform, constructed more than 3,000 years ago. The Romans, who farmed parts of the land, were the first to construct artificial watercourses for both transport and drainage. Nevertheless, in 1066, when the Normans invaded England under William, Duke of Normandy, the peat-lands remained a hostile and swampy wilderness. The islands, however, became places of refuge for those seeking to escape from the world or to avoid persecution. In the case of Hereward the Wake – the son of Leofric, Earl of Mercia, and his wife Godiva – the Isle of Ely (or the Isle of Eels) became an inviolable stronghold from which he and his followers waged guerrilla warfare against the Normans for more than a year: until 1071, in fact, when the Conqueror was shown the hidden route through the Fens by the monks of Ely, who had grown tired of being besieged. Hereward, having managed to escape across the marshes, vanished into obscurity. Legend says that he made peace with William, but was eventually murdered by his Norman enemies.

Piecemeal attempts at improving the drainage in the Fens had been made during the Middle Ages, notably by the monks of Thorney, who, according to the twelfth-century ecclesiastical historian, William of Malmesbury, 'created a paradise' within the marshes, and by John Morton, Bishop of Ely (later Archbishop of Canterbury), who dug a 'leam' to carry the waters of the Nene from Peterborough to Guyhirn, near Wisbech, in the late fifteenth century. Large-scale drainage and reclamation of the wetlands, however, began in the 1630s when Francis, 4th Earl of Bedford, together with a group of wealthy entrepreneurs, or 'Adventurers', commissioned the Dutch drainage engineer Cornelius Vermuyden to construct the Bedford River (now called the Old Bedford River). Some 70 feet wide and 21 miles in length, the cut ran in a straight line from Earith to Denver, with a sluice at each end, and was designed to divert the water from the upper reaches of the Ouse away from its original meandering course around the Isle of Ely. Other drainage canals followed, including the New Bedford (or Hundred Foot) River, the Forty Foot (or Vermuyden's) Drain, and the Twenty Foot River. Linked to these artificial rivers, a complex network of dykes and drains was also created.

The removal of water by various drainage schemes – accelerated by the erection of pumps (first driven by wind, later by steam, oil and electricity) – caused the spongy peat to shrink gradually and the level of the land to sink. In consequence, the water in the embanked drainage channels is now several feet above the level of the surrounding fields. The most dramatic example of peat-shrinkage and land-sinkage, which is still continuing, can be found at Holme Fen, south of Peterborough, where the top of a post, which was level with the surface of the peat in the mid nineteenth century, is now more than 12 feet above the ground. Stacked on the edges of fields in the vicinity of Holme Fen are the preserved trunks of trees that have been dug out of the peat. Known as 'bog oaks', they serve as a reminder that some 6,000 years ago the Fens were once covered by forest.

Today, drainage has turned the fenlands into one of the richest agricultural areas in England. Yet much of the reclaimed land lies below the level of the sea. Inevitably, despite the completion of a massive flood-protection scheme in 1964, serious flooding remains an ever-present threat. A plaque, dated 1830, attached to the Hundred Foot Pump Station, near Pymore, proclaims triumphantly:

These *Fens* have oft-times been by *Water* drown'd/Science a remedy in *Water* found
The power of *Steam* she said shall be employ'd/And the *Destroyer* by *Itself* destroy'd.

Yet, as the devastating floods of 1947 and 1953 confirmed, the destructive power of water cannot be underestimated. Due to sinking coastlines and rising seas, some experts predict that it is simply a matter of time before large tracts of East Anglia are drowned beneath the waves. In the event, Ely would become an island, once again, and the Fens, the 'Land of the Three-quarter Sky', would revert back to their natural state – a vast untamed wilderness of marsh, lake and flood.

Denny Abbey

Denny Abbey, some six miles north-east of Cambridge, was first founded as a priory for a small community of Benedictine monks from Ely in *c.* 1159. During the 1170s the building was acquired by the Knights Templar, who used it as a hospital for old and infirm members of the Order. After the Order's suppression in 1312, the estate passed to the Crown, and in 1327 Edward III granted it to Mary de Valence, the widowed Countess of Pembroke. She, in turn, gave it to the Franciscan nuns (known as Minoresses or Poor Clares) at Waterbeach, nearby, some of whom moved to Denny in 1342. Waterbeach was finally abandoned in 1351 after the rest of the sisters were forced to leave. As the Countess increasingly spent more and more time at Denny, part of the Templar church and infirmary were converted into apartments for her own private use. A new and grander church, of which nothing now survives, was built to the east. After the abbey's dissolution in *c.* 1539 the nave of the Benedictine church was converted into a farmhouse. The sash windows were added in the eighteenth century.

Woolsthorpe Manor

Sir Isaac Newton, one of Britain's greatest scientists, was born at Woolsthorpe Manor, a small seventeenth-century farmhouse seven miles south of Grantham, on 25 December 1642. By the time he was two, his mother – widowed just before his birth – had married the minister Barnabus Smith and moved to a neighbouring village to rear a second family. Young Isaac was left behind at Woolsthorpe in the care of his grandmother. In 1661, having attended the grammar school at Grantham, he became a student at Trinity College, Cambridge, where, four years later, he received a bachelor's degree. Shortly after, the plague closed the university and Newton was forced to return home. During the following two years he formulated most of his major discoveries, including the principle of differential calculus, the understanding that white light is composed of many colours, and the law of universal gravitation. The gnarled old tree in the Manor garden is said to be a descendant of the tree from which Newton watched an apple fall, thereby inspiring his work on gravity.

Lord Burghley's Hospital,
Stamford

Straddling the River Welland at the south-western tip of Lincolnshire and close to the borders of Leicestershire, Northamptonshire and Cambridgeshire, the market town of Stamford originated as a river-crossing settlement at the convergence of numerous ancient roads, including the Roman Ermine Street. During the tenth century it was one of 'five boroughs' within the Danelaw (the area of eastern England settled by the Danes), the others being Leicester, Derby, Lincoln and Nottingham. All were important trading centres and strongholds. After the Norman Conquest, the Anglo-Danish fortress was replaced by a motte-and-bailey castle and during the thirteenth century the town was walled. Since Stamford lies on the oolitic limestone belt that stretches from the Cotswolds to Yorkshire, most of its houses are built of the stone, including Lord Burghley's Hospital. Founded in 1597 and incorporating fragments of the medieval hospital of St Thomas and St John, it is named after William Cecil, 1st Lord Burghley, who also built Burghley House, set in parkland on the outskirts of the town, in 1555-87.

Belton House

Designed in the shape of an H (probably by the Anglo-Dutch architect William Winde), Belton House, near Grantham in Lincolnshire, was built by the master mason, William Stanton, for Sir John Brownlow in 1685-7, and was altered by James Wyatt in the 1770s. It was restored to its original splendour by the 3rd Earl Brownlow during the latter half of the nineteenth century. Generally considered to be the finest Restoration-period house in England, the property – set in magnificent parkland – was acquired by the National Trust in 1984. The rich and opulent English Baroque decoration of the interiors was created by some of the best craftsmen of the period, including the plasterer Edward Goudge and possibly the woodcarver Grinling Gibbons. Among the paintings on display are portraits by Joshua Reynolds (1723-92) and Lord Leighton (1830-96), and huge decorative landscapes by the Dutch artist Melchio de Hondecoeter (1636-95). Before his abdication in 1936, Edward VIII (a close friend of the 6th Lord Brownlow) stayed several times at the house.

Anglesey Abbey

The priory (never an abbey) of Anglesey at Lode, about six miles north-east of Cambridge city centre, was founded for Augustinian canons in *c.* 1212, probably on the site of a monastic hospital. After its dissolution in 1536, the buildings were gradually demolished. Part of the remains, including the thirteenth-century chapter house, was converted into a substantial dwelling in the early seventeenth century, with later modifications and extensions, notably in 1861 and between 1926 and 1958. The American-born Huttleston Broughton, 1st Lord Fairhaven, and his brother, Henry, purchased Anglesey in 1926. Four years later, Lord Fairhaven made the Abbey his main residence. He filled the rooms with a magnificent collection of paintings and furniture, while transforming the surrounding Fenland levels into a 100-acre garden and arboretum, which Sir Arthur Bryant considered to be comparable with 'the great masterpieces of the Georgian era'. The property, including Lode Mill, now belongs to the National Trust.

Peckover House,
Wisbech

According to Pevsner, Peckover House is not only the 'showpiece of Wisbech', it is also situated on 'one of the finest Georgian brick streets of England' – North Brink. Built in 1722, the elegant three-storey town house – overlooking the artificial course of the River Nene – was purchased by the Quaker banker Jonathan Peckover in 1794. Twelve years earlier, he had become associated with the local bank of Gurney, Birkbeck, Peckover and Buxton, which became one of the founder members of Barclays Bank in 1896. Since the family's banking business operated from a wing (since demolished) adjoining their home, it was then known as 'Bank House'. The property, noted for its interior wood and plaster decoration, was given to the National Trust by the Hon. Alexandrina Peckover in 1943. The garden, covering some two acres, is essentially Victorian and includes an orangery and fernery. Octavia Hill, one of the founders of the National Trust, was born at 7-8 South Brink in 1838. A small exhibition on her life and works can be seen in Peckover House.

Walpole St Peter Church

Situated in the small Marshland village of Walpole St Peter, some five miles north-east of Wisbech, the parish church of St Peter – known as the 'Queen of the Marshlands' – is one of the most impressive in Norfolk. All that survives of the old church, washed away by a sea flood in 1337, is the tower, built in c. 1300. The rest of the building is essentially Perpendicular in style, but parts, such as the west window, are Decorated. Large aisle windows, mainly of clear glass, fill the spacious interior of the church with light. Chandeliers hang from the roof of the nave. While a notice in the south porch reminds worshippers to remove their pattens. Curiously, running beneath the raised High Altar of the chancel is a vaulted passage connecting the north and south sides of the churchyard. Among the church fittings are to be found fifteenth- and seventeenth-century benches, a pulpit of about 1605, and a fifteenth-century font inscribed 'Thynk and Thank'. There is also a portable shelter, resembling a sentry-box, for use by the parson at wet or windy funerals.

Peterborough Cathedral

Straddling the River Nene at the western edge of the Cambridgeshire Fens, the city of Peterborough is a 'new town' with an ancient heart – its glorious cathedral. The first abbey at *Medeshamstede* (Peterborough) was founded in 655 by Peada, the first Christian King of Mercia. Sacked by the Danes in 870, the abbey was refounded for Benedictine monks in 960 and dedicated to St Peter. By the end of the century it was surrounded by a defensive wall and *Medeshamstede* (possibly 'homestead by the whirlpool') became Burgh (a fortified place), and later Burgh St Peter, and finally Peterborough. After fire destroyed the abbey in 1116, Abbot John de Sais began to build the present church, which was not completed until 1238. Further rebuilding included the replacement of the Norman tower with one in the Decorated style in c. 1335. In 1541, two years after the dissolution of the abbey, the church was saved and made a cathedral. The tomb of Catherine of Aragon, Henry VIII's first wife, is in the North Presbytery Aisle.

Boston Stump

William Cobbett visited the medieval Fenland port and market town of Boston in April 1830 and wrote in *Rural Rides*: 'The great pride and glory of the Bostonians is *their church*, which . . . has a tower 300 feet high, which is both a landmark and a sea-mark. To describe the richness, the magnificence, the symmetry, the exquisite beauty of this pile is wholly out of my power.' Although the fifteenth-century lantern tower of the 'wool' church of St Botolph is affectionately known as the 'Stump', the origin of its name is uncertain: some say that it refers to the steeple's distant appearance; others claim that it should have carried a spire and was, therefore, never finished. The steps to the top of the tower – 272 feet in height from ground level to the very tip of the weather vanes – are reputed to number 365, one for every day of the year. The main structure of the present church was begun in 1309. Measuring 282 feet in length and 100 feet in width, it is one of the largest parish churches in England. The name 'Boston' is popularly said to derive from 'Botolph's town'.

Holme Fen

Holme Fen nature reserve, with its birch woodland and flooded pits formed by peat extraction, stands on the south-western edge of Whittlesey Mere, south of Peterborough. Once covering 2,000 acres of low-lying fenland, the mere was one of the largest freshwater lakes in southern Britain. In 1848, three years before it was completely drained, a timber post was driven through the soil into the underlying clay at Holme Fen to measure the rate of peat shrinkage. In 1851 the post was replaced by a cast iron pillar, reputedly from the Great Exhibition at Crystal Palace. Originally level with the surface of the peat, the top of the post is now more than 12 feet above the ground. A second post, erected in 1957, shows the drop in ground level at various dates. Since the land around Holme Fen is nine feet below sea-level, it is also the lowest-lying area in Britain. Among the items discovered on the bed of Whittlesey Mere after it had been drained was the 'Ramsey Abbey Censer' and 'Incense Boat', dating from *c.* 1325 and now housed in London's Victoria and Albert Museum.

Wicken Fen,
near Soham

The first tract of wetland at Wicken Fen – which came to the National Trust piecemeal and includes Sedge Fen and Adventurers' Fen – was purchased in 1899, making it Britain's oldest nature reserve and one of the few surviving remnants of undrained fenland in East Anglia. Sedge Fen, a popular collecting ground for nineteenth-century entomologists, has never been drained and, therefore, stands islanded several feet above the rich black soil of the surrounding farmland. The small wooden smock drainage mill, reconstructed on its present site in 1956, is the last surviving working windpump in Cambridgeshire. By pumping water *into* rather than *out of* the fen, it helps to maintain water levels and protect the spongy peat from drying out. To retain the traditional balance between the various wetland habitats, the beds and fields are regularly harvested: the reed and sedge are used for thatching; while the litter (once cut for hay) is gathered and burned. Fen Cottage, build with traditional Fenland materials, is furnished as it would have been in the 1930s.

Sibsey Trader Mill

Built in 1877 by Saundersons, millwrights of Louth, the brick tower mill at Sibsey – five miles north of Boston – is one of very few six-sailed windmills to survive in England. The use of more than four sails to increase the power and efficiency of the mill was widely adopted in Lincolnshire from the late eighteenth century onwards. The Maud Foster Mill at Boston, for example, has five sails. Built in 1819 by Norman and Smithson of Hull, this seven-storey structure is the tallest working windmill in England. The only eight-sailed windmill to survive in Britain is the tower mill at Heckington, 11 miles west of Boston. All three mills have the typical Lincolnshire ogee-shaped cap. The tapering six-storey tower of the Sibsey Trader Mill is tarred outside and whitewashed inside. Its wrought-iron balcony on the second floor gave the miller access to the chain-and-weight mechanism that adjusted the shutters of the sails, thereby governing their speed. Since the tower is fixed, the eight-bladed fantail turns the cap to face the wind.

Nene Outfall Cut,
near Sutton Bridge

Rising on the hills south of Daventry, the Nene flows north-eastward for 110 miles before entering The Wash beyond Sutton Bridge in Lincolnshire. The course of the river, however, has changed considerably since medieval times. Today, as a part of England's inland waterway network, it is navigable for more than 90 miles. Large-scale work on the drainage and reclamation of the Fenlands began in the 1630s with the construction of the Old Bedford River. Other drainage canals followed, including the New Bedford (or Hundred Foot) River, completed in 1651. At about the same time, a sluice was erected at Stan-ground, near Peterborough, to control the flow of the Nene into Morton's Leam (cut in the late fifteenth century). Since 1728, however, when a new channel was completed between Peter-borough and Guyhirn, the main waters of the Nene have flowed through the River Nene Cut. The Nene Outfall Cut was completed in 1830. In 1216, while trying to cross the Nene estuary near Sutton Bridge, King John's baggage train was overwhelmed by the incoming tide and his treasure lost.

Tulip Fields,
near Walpole Cross Keys

The silt-lands bordering The Wash – which include Marshland (that part of Norfolk between Wisbech and the Great Ouse) and the Lincolnshire district of South Holland – contain some of the richest farming soils in Britain. Although the commonest crops are wheat, barley, sugar beet and potatoes, the area is probably best known for its colourful fields of tulips and daffodils. As a by-product of bulb production, most of the flowers are used to decorate carnival floats at the Spalding spring festival parade. Millions are needed, for to cover one square yard of a float takes as many as a thousand flower-heads. Many of the churches are also decorated with flowers during the festival. The old sea wall near Walpole Cross Keys in Marshland was built to reduce the risk of flooding. When it was constructed is uncertain: tradition suggests a Roman origin; Anglo-Saxon place names point to a date before the Norman Conquest; while some experts claim it is medieval. The reclaimed land to the seaward side of the bank is higher because tidal deposits of silt and mud had longer to accumulate.

KING'S LYNN AND WEST NORFOLK

Thornham Channel, *Thornham*

Once on the edge of the sea and now almost a mile inland, the village of Thornham dates back at least to Anglo-Saxon times, and possibly earlier. Aerial photographs, taken in 1948, revealed a small Iron Age fort south-west of the village (used as a burial ground in the sixth and seventh centuries). The arrival of the Black Death in 1348 – reputedly brought from King's Lynn by infected fleas in a piece of cloth – not only decimated the population, but also brought the rebuilding of the church of All Saints to an abrupt halt. A scale model of the 'composite' windmill, which once stood on the brick base tower near the harbour, can be found in the church. In order to drain the marshes beyond Holme-Next-the-Sea, the River Hun was diverted towards Thornham. In consequence, Holme harbour silted up and Thornham took over its trade. Thornham's harbour, in turn, declined with the arrival of the railway at Hunstanton in 1862. Thornham Channel marks the eastern extremity of the Holme Dunes nature reserve.

From the silt-lands of The Wash – beyond King's Lynn, one of medieval England's foremost ports – the coast of Norfolk sweeps in a huge bulge, first north, then east and finally south. Between the cliffs of Hunstanton and Weybourne, the low-lying coastline is made up of an ever-changing landscape of salt-marshes, shingle ridges, sand dunes and mudflats. Known as the 'North Alluvial Plain', this 25-mile strip of land is bounded inland by the former coastline. In addition to being both an official 'Area of Outstanding Natural Beauty' and a Heritage Coast, it is internationally renowned for the richness and variety of its bird life.

Between Holme-Next-the-Sea and Salthouse, there is an almost unbroken series of nature reserves, owned or administered by the National Trust, the Royal Society for the Protection of Birds, the Nature Conservancy Council and the Norfolk Naturalists Trust. Further east, at Weybourne, the soft crumbling cliffs climb steadily past the seaside resorts of Sheringham and Cromer, through 'Poppyland', and on to Mundesley. Beyond Happisburgh, where the cliffs sink under sand dunes, the coast curves southwards to Caister-on-Sea and Great Yarmouth. Since much of the land between Happisburgh and Winterton-on-Sea is below the high-water mark, all that prevents the sea from flooding into the Broads is a single sea wall capped by dunes and stabilized by plants such as marram grass, which has long, binding roots. In order to safeguard the structural stability of the wall, however, a massive coastal defence programme was launched in 1994, involving the construction of a series of offshore 'reefs'. Once they are completed, it is hoped that these long-term measures will ensure that the foreshore levels of sand and shingle are retained and, as a result, they will continue to act as a protective barrier between the sea and the existing wall.

Inland, unlike the neighbouring Cambridgeshire and Lincolnshire Fens, Norfolk is not flat. The highest part of the county is to be found at the 'Holt-Cromer Ridge', which is formed of gravels, sands and clays deposited during the last Ice Age. Running approximately east-west, it reaches a height of about 340 feet on Beacon Hill, near the coastal village of West Runton. At its north-eastern seaward end, the ridge terminates in the cliffs of Weybourne and Cromer. While its south-western slopes merge gently into the rolling uplands of the 'Good Sands' (so named because the light glacial soils were 'good' by the farming standards of the eighteenth century). It was here, from the late seventeenth century onwards, that dramatic improvements on a national scale were made in food production, notably by Thomas William Coke (1754-1842), 1st Earl of Leicester of the 2nd creation, who inherited the Holkham estate in 1776. Although a Member of Parliament for 50 years, 'Coke of Holkham', or 'Coke of Norfolk', is best remembered for his agricultural achievements, which included the new system of farming known as the 'Norfolk husbandry'. This made a fallow year unnecessary by including clover, or other fodder plants, in a four-course rotation of crops.

In stark contrast to the rich fertility of the 'Good Sands' and, indeed, to the rest of the Norfolk, the sandy soils of the Breckland are extremely poor in terms of fertility. Named after its 'brecks', or tracts of once-cultivated heathland, this area of south-west Norfolk and north-west Suffolk is one of the driest parts of all England. About 4,000 years ago, during Neolithic times, the light soils and thin woodlands were not only cleared to provide small arable fields, but the bands of flint in the underlying chalk were exploited to make primitive tools and weapons. At Grimes Graves, one of the earliest industrial sites in Britain, the Neolithic or New Stone Age miners dug pits as deep as 40 feet in order to extract the deposits of flint. Within an area of some 92 acres, it is estimated that there were almost 400 deep mines, linked to each other by underground galleries radiating out from the shafts and following the bands of flint. For centuries, the origin of the curious cup-shaped hollows that pitted the desolate heathland was unknown. The mystery was finally solved in 1870, however, when excavation established that the grass-covered hollows were the tops of infilled mine-shafts. The name 'Grime's Graves', however, does not refer to a burial ground, but it is derived from the Anglo-Saxon for 'Grim's quarries' or the 'Devil's holes'.

In the west of the county, in the region separating the 'Good Sands' from the silt- and peat-lands of the Fens, is a low escarpment, known as the 'Greensand Belt'. The scarp is not continuous, however, but has been divided into distinct blocks by the courses of several rivers. The Nar, for example, on its winding westerly course to King's Lynn and The Wash, has carved out a valley that is almost two miles wide near Setchey. The watershed between the rivers that flow westward into The Wash (the Babingley, Nar, Wissey, Thet and Little Ouse) and those that flow in the opposite direction to the North Sea (the Wensum, Yare and Waveney) is formed by the chalk uplands that stretch diagonally from Hunstanton to Watton. A second, and shorter, watershed running at right angles to the former, occurs along the high ground of the 'Holt-Cromer Ridge'. From this region, the waters of the Bure flow south-eastward, while those of the Stiffkey and Glaven flow in a northerly direction.

The River Great Ouse, fed by a complicated network of smaller rivers and drainage channels, rises in the Midlands, flows through the neat black fields of the Cambridgeshire Fens before entering The Wash at King's Lynn. Originally, the river (which joined the Nene) emptied into the sea through a vast natural estuary in the vicinity of present-day Wisbech. The diversion of the Great Ouse to King's Lynn in the thirteenth century secured the town's position as a major port for the export and import of goods to and from the markets of eastern and central England, which contained some of the richest farmlands in the country.

In October 1216, incidentally, during his campaign to recover East Anglia from the barons, King John contracted dysentery at King's Lynn, brought on by fatigue and over-indulgence in food and drink. While the king and his army travelled to Newark in Lincolnshire, by way of Wisbech, his baggage train (laden with treasure) took the shorter route across the salt-marshes of The Wash. Unfortunately, the entire convoy – wagons, men and horses – were either overwhelmed by the incoming tide or swallowed up in quicksands and were lost. Almost immediately after hearing of the tragedy, John died. His treasure has never been found.

When Defoe visited King's Lynn in the early eighteenth century, he found it 'rich, populous and thriving'. Adding, in *A Tour Thro' the Whole Island of Great Britain:*

> 'It is a beautiful well-built, and well-situated town, at the mouth of the River Ouse, and has this particular attending it, which gives it a vast advantage in trade; namely, that there is the greatest extent of inland navigation here, of any port in England, London excepted. The reason whereof is this, that there are more navigable rivers empty themselves here into the sea, including the Washes which are branches of the same port, than at any one mouth of waters in England, except the Thames and Humber. By these navigable rivers the merchants of Lynn supply about six counties wholly, and three counties in part, with their goods which has given rise to this observation on the town of Lynn, that they bring in more coals, than any sea-port between London and Newcastle; and import more wines than any port in England, except London and Bristol.'

During the nineteenth century, in addition to straightening and altering the course of the Great Ouse estuary, new docks and warehouses were built to increase the port's shipping capacity. Further improvements, including the completion of the 'Riverside Quay' development in 1992, have helped to maintain King's Lynn's ancient and historic role, not only as a busy commercial port, but also as one of the largest and most important towns in west Norfolk.

Custom House,
King's Lynn

Situated on the banks of the River Great Ouse, King's Lynn was one of medieval England's chief ports and trading centres. Lynn, as it is often called, was originally two towns: Bishop's Lynn (founded in *c.* 1100 by Bishop Herbert de Losinga) and the 'New Land' (laid out some 50 years later). 'Lynn' means 'lake' or 'pool'. Both towns remained distinct until King John's charter of 1204; while Henry VIII changed the name to 'Lynn Regis' or 'King's Lynn'. Among the many fine buildings in the port is the Custom House on Purfleet Quay, built as a Merchants' Exchange in 1683. Henry Bell, the architect, is also reputed to have remodelled the front of nearby Clifton House, one of the town's oldest merchant's houses, with parts dating back to the twelfth century. Its five-storeyed, Elizabethan brick watchtower overlooks the waterfront. St George's Guildhall, built in the early fifteenth century, is the largest surviving medieval guildhall in England. Near the Custom House is the decaying hulk of the schooner *Dania*, built at Svenborg, Denmark, in 1903.

Windmill,
Great Bircham

Built in 1846, the tower windmill at Great Bircham ceased grinding corn in 1930 and, nine years later, became part of the Sandringham Estate. In 1975 the derelict building was purchased by Roger Wagg, the great grandson of Joseph Wagg, who owned the property in the latter half of the nineteenth century. The mill has now been restored to full working order. On open days, visitors can climb the five floors up to the fan stage, while savouring the smell of freshly baked bread coming out of the small bakery attached to the mill building. They can also watch the bread being baked in the 200-year-old coal-fired peel oven. One of a group of three Birchams, the village of Great Bircham contains a fourteenth-century church with Norman fragments. Church Farm (formerly the parsonage), opposite the church at Bircham Newton, was the home in 1825-30 of Horatia, the illegitimate daughter of Lord Nelson and Lady Hamilton. All that remains of the church at Bircham Tofts is an ivy-covered ruin.

Creake Abbey,
North Creake

The monastery at North Creake was first founded as a small hospital and almshouses towards the end of the twelfth century. In 1206 it was refounded by Sir Robert and Lady Alice de Nerford, and subsequently turned into an Augustinian priory. In 1231, under the patronage of Henry III, the house was granted abbey status with the right to elect its own abbot. A fire in 1484, reputed to have been started deliberately, destroyed much of the church and the cloister buildings. Unable to raise the finance to rebuild, it was decided to salvage what remained of the church by blocking off the chancel and demolishing the nave and transepts. A worse tragedy struck not long afterwards, however, when plague killed all of the canons, with the exception of the abbot. When he eventually died in 1506, the abbey was dissolved and the property reverted to its patron, the Crown. Soon after, the revenues were transferred to Christ's College, Cambridge. Part of the ruined buildings has been converted into a farmhouse.

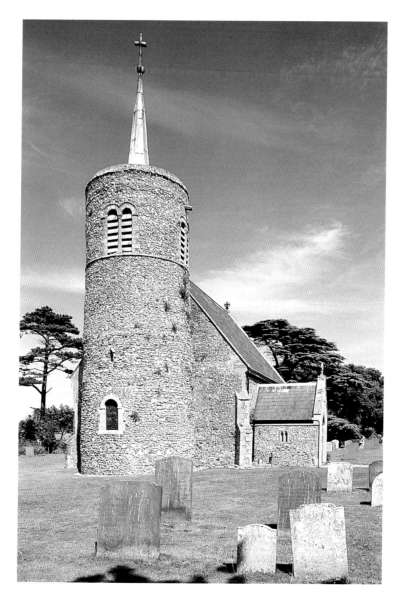

Church of St Mary the Virgin,
Titchwell

Due to its cheapness, abundance and the ease with which it can be split into shapes, flint has been used as a building material in both Norfolk and Suffolk since Roman times. Many of the houses and cottages along the North Norfolk coast, for example, are constructed of rounded flint pebbles gathered locally, and held in place by mortar. Since it is difficult to form strong angles with flint, doorways, windows and corners are invariably made with dressed stone or bricks. The flint bell tower of Titchwell parish church, like many erected during the Anglo-Saxon period, is round, thereby avoiding corners altogether. Mentioned in the Domesday survey of 1086, the church was extensively reconstructed in the Perpendicular style during the fifteenth century. Further restoration was carried out in Victorian times, and the thatched roof of the nave was replaced with one of slate. To the north of the village, Titchwell Marsh, covering some 420 acres, is one of two reserves on the North Norfolk coast owned by the Royal Society for the Protection of Birds.

Chapel,
North Elmham

First established at Dunwich by St Felix in *c.* 630, the Bishopric of East Anglia was transferred to North Elmham in *c.* 673, where it remained until it was moved to Thetford in *c.* 1075. The first cathedral at Elmham, six miles north of East Dereham, was built of timber. Whether it was rebuilt in stone during the Anglo-Saxon period, however, is uncertain. After ceasing to be a cathedral, the building remained in use as a parish church until *c.* 1100, when the church of St Mary was erected nearby by Bishop Herbert de Losinga. The former cathedral was then demolished and replaced by a stone chapel for the bishop's private use. In the fourteenth century the chapel was converted into a fortified dwelling by Bishop Henry le Despencer. The entrance was raised from the ground floor to the first floor, and the semicircular stair turret duplicated on the opposite side of the doorway. Access to the 'castle' (surrounded by defensive earthworks) was by way of a drawbridge across a dry moat. The ruins are now in the care of English Heritage.

Cliffs at Hunstanton

The 60-foot-high cliffs at Hunstanton, overlooking The Wash, are famous for their horizontally striped layers of carstone and chalk, ranging in colour from gingerbread to white. Millions of years ago, in the area now occupied by Norfolk, cataclysmic movements of the earth's crust caused the sedimentary layers of Cretaceous beds to tilt or slope from west to east. The white chalk, therefore, forms the top of the cliffs at Hunstanton, the base of those at Weybourne, while at Great Yarmouth it lies some 500 feet below sea-level. On top of the cliffs at Old Hunstanton, near the disused lighthouse, are fragments of a chapel built in 1272 by the Benedictine monks of Bury St Edmunds to commemorate the East Anglian king and martyr St Edmund. Legend says that, after crossing the sea from Germany, he landed here to claim his 'God-given' kingdom in 855. The seaside resort of New Hunstanton, south of St Edmund's Point, developed after the arrival of the railway in 1862. It is the only resort in East Anglia to face west towards the setting sun.

Common Place,
Little Walsingham

Before is destruction in 1536, the shrine at Our Lady of Walsingham was one of the most revered places of pilgrimage in England. So many people undertook the journey to the tiny Norfolk village that even the Milky Way galaxy – said to light the route to the shrine across the heavens – became known as the Walsingham Way. Almost every monarch from Henry III to Henry VIII travelled to Little Walsingham – 'England's Nazareth' – to pay their respects, some returning many times. Today the village, with its ancient inns, half-timbered houses and narrow alleyways, is a mecca for pilgrims and tourists alike. The brick pump house, in the market square (called the Common Place), dates from the sixteenth century, and covers the village's ancient well. The brazier on its top is thought to have been used to provide general illumination for the square as well as a light for those drawing water. Nearby are the ruins of the Augustinian priory (called Walsingham Abbey), the original site of the shrine.

Castle Acre Priory

The Cluniac Order was introduced into England in 1077 by William de Warenne, 1st Earl of Surrey, and his wife Gundrada. Although its early history is obscure, the Cluniac priory at Castle Acre is thought to have been founded by William's son, the 2nd Earl of Surrey, in 1090. Although it was first sited within the castle precincts, the priory was soon moved to the low-lying valley of the River Nar, about a quarter of a mile south-west of the village. Dissolved in 1537, the remains (like the castle) are now in the care of English Heritage. On the left of the photograph can be seen the west front of the church and, in the centre, the prior's lodgings. A few miles downstream are the remains of an Augustinian priory, founded in the twelfth century. The present village of Castle Acre was originally a small medieval walled town, laid out within the outer bailey of the castle. Standing by the village green (known as Stocks Green), the Bailey Gate was built in the thirteenth century to defend the town's northern entrance.

River Burn,
Burnham Overy

Burnham Overy is one of seven villages that take the first part of their name from the little River Burn. The most westerly, Burnham Deepdale, has a church with a round flint tower dating from the late Anglo-Saxon period. Its principal glory is the twelfth-century stone font, carved with farming scenes representing each month of the year, three of which, surprisingly, depict inactivity indoors. The church of St Margaret of Antioch at Burnham Norton also has a round tower but, because of its improved construction, it is thought to date from about 1090. The three settlements of Burnham Sutton, Burnham Ulph and Burnham Westgate now form the largest of the Burnhams – Burnham Market. Burnham Thorpe is celebrated as Nelson's birthplace. Burnham Overy Town was once a busy seaport, but the silting up of the river caused Burnham Overy Staithe to be built nearer the coast. The cottages in the photograph (one with horseshoes set in the wall) lie midway between Overy Town and Overy Staithe, near a late eighteenth-century watermill.

Caley Mill,
Heacham

The lavender farm at Caley Mill, Heacham, was started by two men: Linn Chilvers, a nurseryman; and Francis 'Ginger' Dusgate of nearby Fring Hall. It was not until 1935, however, three years after they first went into partnership growing lavender, that Dusgate purchased Caley Mill – the headquarters of Norfolk Lavender Ltd. Up until 1964, when the first mechanical cutter was introduced, the lavender flowers were harvested by hand using sickle-shaped knives. The present purpose-built machine is forty times more productive, able to harvest four acres of lavender a day. Depending on the weather, harvesting lasts for about five to six weeks, usually starting in the middle of July, when the oil yield is at its peak, and the air is thick with the scent of flowers and the sound of bees. Although lavender is grown at Caley Mill, where a National Collection of Lavenders has been established, the main plantations are found in the surrounding countryside.

Gatehouse,
Burnham Norton Friary

One of more than 150 religious houses in medieval Norfolk, the Carmelite friary at Burnham Norton was begun in 1242-7 and dissolved in 1538. Neither large nor important, it was nevertheless the first foundation of the Carmelites (or White Friars) in the county. The Order originated in the late twelfth century when a community of hermits settled on Mount Carmel in Palestine. They were driven out of the Holy Land, however, by the Muslims in 1238 and, although a new base was established in Cyprus, some returned to England. In 1247, at a General Chapter held at Aylesford in Kent, the Carmelites decided to become friars rather than hermits, and to make their Order mendicant (which meant that although they would continue to live together and obey vows, as monks do, they were able to go out into the world, to preach, to serve the people and to cater for their needs). Among the sparse remains to survive at Burnham Norton friary are the fourteenth-century gatehouse and the west wall of the church.

All Saints' Church,
Burnham Thorpe

Lord Horatio Nelson was born on 29 September 1758 in the old rectory at Burnham Thorpe. His father, Edmund, moved to the village in 1775 and was rector not only of Burnham Thorpe, but also of Burnham Norton, Burnham Sutton and Burnham Ulph. He died in 1802 and was buried in All Saints' church. 'Nelson's Church', as it has come to be known, originally formed the centre of the medieval settlement of Burnham Thorpe. After the Black Death reached England in 1348, however, the village was moved further away: thereby accounting for the fact that the site of the old rectory (which was demolished in 1803) is more than half a mile south of the church. Nelson was killed at the battle of Trafalgar in 1805 and his body was brought back to England, preserved in a cask of rum. Although he gloried in being a Norfolk man and expected to be buried alongside his parents in the church where he was christened, he was, in fact, laid to rest in St Paul's Cathedral, London. Two years later, The Plough public house situated at Burnham Thorpe was renamed the Lord Nelson.

Keep and Gatehouse,
Castle Rising

Surrounded by a circle of formidable earthworks, the keep at Castle Rising was built by William de Albini (later Earl of Sussex) in c. 1138, the year that he married Adela of Louvain, widow of Henry I. The earthworks and gatehouse were erected at around the same time. In addition to being a defensive stronghold, the keep was also designed to provide residential accommodation for the lord and his immediate retinue. Noted for its richly decorated forebuilding, the keep is a 'hall' keep, rather than the more usual 'tower' keep (in other words, it is broader than it is high). During the thirteenth century, the castle passed to the Montalt family and, in 1331, to the Crown, becoming one of the residences of Isabella, widow of Edward II, until her death in 1358. Within the inner bailey, to the north of the keep, are the remains of a Norman church, dating from the late eleventh century. It is thought to have been the original parish church of the village, abandoned and replaced by the present church when the castle was founded.

Parish Church,
Swaffham

The parish church of St Peter and St Paul at Swaffham was rebuilt in Perpendicular style between 1454 and 1490; while the tower, with its spire of 1897, was added in 1507-10. On the ends of the front pews – beneath the magnificent double hammerbeam roof of the nave, decorated with 88 carved angels with wings outstretched – are figures of John Chapman (known as the Pedlar of Swaffham) and his dog. According to legend, Chapman (a real person) dreamed that if he went to London Bridge he would learn something that would make his fortune. Wasting no time, he found himself on the bridge telling a shopkeeper about his dream. The man laughed and said that only fools believed in such nonsense, adding that he himself had recently dreamed that treasure lay buried under a tree in the garden of a Swaffham man called Chapman. Returning home, Chapman dug up two pots of gold and, with his new-found wealth, financed the building of the north aisle and other parts of the church in c. 1462.

St Mary's Priory,
Binham

The Benedictine priory at Binham, five miles south-east of Wells-Next-the-Sea, was founded as a cell of St Albans Abbey by Peter de Valoines, Lord of Orford, in c. 1091. Although the main structure of the church is Norman, the west front is Early English – and, if it was constructed between 1226 and 1244 (the dates indicated by the medieval chronicler Matthew Paris), then it is the earliest of its kind in the whole of England. Likewise, the great window contains one of the country's earliest examples of bar, or geometrical, tracery, which originated earlier in the century at Rheims Cathedral in France. Today, unfortunately, most of the window has been bricked in. After the priory's dissolution in 1539, seven of the original nine bays of the nave were converted to serve as the parish church, and the rest of the building demolished. The extensive remains of the monastic buildings, which include the ruins of the crossing and eastern end of the church, are now in the care of English Heritage.

Slipper Chapel,
Houghton St Giles

According to legend, Richeldis de Favarches, a noblewoman, had a vision in which she was transported to the scene of the Annunciation (the house in Nazareth where Mary received the angelic news that she was to give birth to Jesus). In 1061, fulfilling what she believed to be a command from the Virgin herself, Richeldis built at Walsingham an exact copy of the 'Holy House', which soon became an important centre of pilgrimage. Before leaving for the Holy Land some 30 years later, her son, Geoffrey, made sure the 'house' and its statue of the Virgin and Child were looked after by instructing his clerk, Edwy, to establish a religious community on the site. In c. 1153 it became a house of Augustinian canons, known as the Priory of the Annunciation of the Blessed Virgin Mary. Pilgrims to 'England's Nazareth' often stopped at Houghton St Giles to remove their shoes and walk the last mile to Walsingham barefoot. The mid-fourteenth-century 'Slipper Chapel' became the Roman Catholic National Shrine of Our Lady of Walsingham in 1934.

'Antique Lamps',
Stiffkey

Situated on the main coast road between Blakeney and Wells-Next-the-Sea, the little village of Stiffkey takes its name from the river that links it to Warham, Wighton, Little Walsingham, Houghton St Giles and Great Snoring. Like many of the coastal villages in Norfolk, Stiffkey lost its harbour and quay because of silting and is now separated from the sea by a large expanse of salt-marsh. During medieval times the village was divided into two manors with two separate churches occupying the same churchyard. Today, only the Perpendicular church of St John the Baptist survives. The village sign, which also bears Stiffkey's alternative name 'Stewkey', depicts women gathering the famous blue-shelled cockles, known as 'Stewkey Blues'. On certain nights it is said that the cries of one woman, drowned by the incoming tide, can be heard across the marshes. The cottage in the photograph forms part of a shop specializing in antique lamps of solid brass dating from about 1880 to 1920.

Wheat and Wild Flowers,
Ringstead

In the 'Good Sands' region of north-west Norfolk the soils are typically light, the farms large (more than 300 acres) and the fields wide with few hedgerows. Chalk, the underlying rock of the county, comes to the surface in the vicinity of Ringstead and Hunstanton (unusually, in the cliffs of the latter it has been coloured red by iron compounds). In fields where pesticides and herbicides have not been used, the ripening corn is ablaze with an incredible variety of wild flowers, including poppies, ox-eye daisies and cornflowers. Although much of the land has been cultivated – wheat and barley being the main cereal crops – areas of chalk grassland still survive. One of the largest, covering an area of about 25 acres, is the Ringstead Downs nature reserve, managed by the Norfolk Naturalists Trust. Traditionally, the grassland would have been grazed by sheep and cattle to prevent the spread of young trees and shrubs. Instead, it is mowed.

St Mary's Priory,
Thetford

During the Middle Ages, Thetford was an ecclesiastical centre of some renown, boasting more than 20 parish churches and at least 11 religious houses, including six hospitals. The most important and the wealthiest was the Cluniac priory of St Mary, founded by Roger Bigod in 1103-4. Its first church occupied the cathedral, vacated when the see moved from Thetford to Norwich in 1094. Due to lack of space, a new monastery was begun on the site of the present remains in 1107. Although the new church was consecrated in 1114, building continued throughout the twelfth century. The Lady Chapel was added in the early thirteenth century. Thomas Howard, 2nd Duke of Norfolk, who defeated the Scots at Flodden in 1513, was buried in the priory church in 1524. The fact that Henry VIII's illegitimate son, Henry Fitzroy, Duke of Richmond, was also buried there in 1536, did not prevent the king from dissolving the priory in 1540. The remains are now in the care of English Heritage. So, too, are the separate ruins of the Augustinian priory of the Holy Sepulchre and Thetford Warren Lodge.

Blakeney Quay

During medieval times, Blakeney was alternatively referred to as Snitterley (the name recorded in the Domesday survey of 1086), but whether they were the same or two distinct places is uncertain. Some suggest that if Snitterley was a separate village, it was washed away by the sea. What is known for certain, however, is that by the thirteenth century Blakeney, Cley and Wiveton were thriving ports (known as the Glaven ports, after the river), with ships up to 150 tons loading and unloading their cargo at the wharfs. Today, because of silting, Blakeney Haven can be used only by small craft. The huge bank of shingle that helps to protect Blakeney and its neighbouring villages from the sea runs westward from Cley to form the three-mile-long spit known as Blakeney Point – a nature reserve famous for its breeding populations of terns and colonies of common and grey seals. Cley Marshes is Britain's oldest county nature reserve: its purchase in 1926 leading to the formation of the Norfolk Naturalists Trust.

Pier and Beach,
Cromer

Once inland and now on the edge of the sea, the town and holiday resort of Cromer – famous for its crabs – developed out of the medieval port of Shipden, which disappeared beneath the waves in the four-teenth and fifteenth centuries. The site of the church of Shipden-juxta-Mare is thought to be about 1,300 feet off the end of the present pier (opened in 1901). Known as 'Church Rock', the remains of the tower were struck by the paddle steamer *Victoria* in 1888, and subse-quently blown up. Permission to erect a new church in the Perpendicular style on the site of an older foundation at Shipden-juxta-Felbrigg (Cromer) was granted by Edward III in 1337. The building, dedicated to St Peter and St Paul, was completed during the reign of Henry IV (1399-1413), and boasts the tallest tower of any parish church in Norfolk, standing 160 feet high. Although the town had become a fashionable bathing resort by the end of the eighteenth century, its greatest development took place after the arrival of the railway in 1877.

Sandringham

In February 1862, some two months after the sudden death of her husband, Prince Albert, Queen Victoria purchased the Sandringham estate for her eldest son, Albert Edward, Prince of Wales (later King Edward VII). The original house, built in the latter half of the eighteenth century, was subse-quently demolished and replaced by a new house designed in the Jacobean style by AJ Humbert, and completed in 1870. The conservatory of the old house, however, was preserved as a bil-liard room (to which the prince added a bowling-alley). As well as replanting the grounds, the lake near the house was filled in and two new lakes excavated further to the south (the Upper Lake is featured in the photo-graph). Further rebuilding of the house was undertaken during restoration caused by a major fire in 1891. Today, the house and grounds stand at the heart of a Royal estate that covers more than 20,000 acres and embraces seven villages and a Country Park (designated in 1968). Since 1977, when the Royal Family are not in residence, Sandringham has been open to the public.

Oxburgh Hall,
Oxborough

Once situated on an island surrounded by undrained marshland, Oxburgh Hall has been the home of the Bedingfeld family for more than 500 years. The present moated house was begun by Sir Edmund Bedingfeld in 1482, the same year that Edward IV granted him permission to fortify the hall with towers and battlements. The royal charter, complete with the Great Seal of England, is on display in the King's Room (the room in which Henry VII slept when he visited the house in 1497). The Queen's Room, named after Elizabeth of York, the King's wife, contains a huge tapestry map of 1647 depicting Oxfordshire and surrounding counties. Some of the embroideries in the Tapestry Room were made by Mary Queen of Scots (1542-87) during her long imprisonment in England. Other features of interest are the Tudor Gatehouse, the sixteenth-century Priest's Hole and the Bedingfeld Chantry Chapel, attached to the partly ruined parish church of Oxborough. Although Oxburgh Hall is owned by the National Trust, it is still lived in by the Bedingfelds.

Blickling Hall

Standing on the site of a moated manor, dating from the end of the fourteenth century, the Jacobean mansion at Blickling was built between 1619 and 1629 by Robert Lyminge for Sir Henry Hobart, a successful and wealthy lawyer who became Lord Chief Justice of the Common Pleas in 1611. Part of the original building – which had been the childhood home of Anne Boleyn, ill-fated second queen of Henry VIII – survived until the 1760s, when the house was extensively remodelled by John Hobart, 2nd Earl of Buckinghamshire. Fortunately, the architects, Thomas and William Ivory, sympathetically preserved the Jacobean character of the country house by making sure that any new building was in harmony with the old. The most impressive room in the house is, without doubt, the Jacobean Long Gallery, 123 feet in length and boasting an elaborate plasterwork ceiling by Edward Stanyon, dating from 1620. Now owned by the National Trust, the Blickling estate, covering 4,800 acres, is also noted for its magnificent wooded parkland, long artificial lake and Victorian sunken garden.

Felbrigg Hall

Surrounded by extensive woods and parkland, Felbrigg Hall was bequeathed to the National Trust in 1969 by the Norfolk historian, RW Ketton-Cremer. During the Middle Ages, the manor was owned by the de Felbrigg family, who are commemorated in the parish church of St Margaret (which they built) by many fine brasses. The village of Felbrigg originally surrounded the church, but at some unknown date was rebuilt on its present site, half a mile to the north-east. In *c.* 1450 the estate was acquired by the Windhams, but after the Norfolk line of the family died out in 1599, it passed to relatives in Somerset. Between *c.* 1620 and 1624 the house was rebuilt by Thomas Windham (originally spelled Wyndham). In huge stone letters along the balustrading are the words: *GLORIA DEO IN EXCELSIS* ('Glory to God in the Highest'). The west wing was added in 1674-87, the Orangery in *c.* 1705 and the east service wing, with its cupola and clock, in 1751-6. Further remodelling, particularly to the great hall, occurred in the nineteenth century.

SS *Vina*, *Brancaster*

Jutting out of the sands at Brancaster Bay, about a mile offshore and just west of Scolt Head Island, are the broken remains of the *SS Vina*, built in 1894. During the Second World War, the aged vessel was pressed into service at Great Yarmouth as a naval 'blockship' (a ship on standby to act as a barrier should enemy vessels threaten to invade the harbour). Throughout the war – despite occupying a dangerously prominent position on the Gorleston side of the River Yare, opposite the navy's main petrol dump – the *Vina* escaped damage from enemy bombardment. During a scare, the ship was towed into position at the harbour entrance and wired with explosives, but, each time, the danger failed to materialize and she was safely returned to her berth. In 1943, alas, she was moved to Brancaster, where the RAF used her as a target ship. Today the *Vina* is considered to be a local menace due to the number of people who have crossed the treacherous channel to get to the wreck and have either drowned or been caught by the incoming tide – which is known to sweep in faster than a man can run.

Sand Dunes,
near Holme-Next-the-Sea

Although the largest areas of sand dunes in Britain mostly occur on the exposed westerly coasts, extensive stretches can be found in the east, notably in North Norfolk between Hunstanton and Sheringham. Formed by the gradual accumulation of wind-blown sands, the dunes are invariably stabilized by marram grass (*Ammophila arenaria*) – the dune builder *par excellence*. With its long, tough and binding roots, the grass is not only able to survive in the harsh environment of the dunes, but is actively encouraged to grow upwards by the continual build-up of fresh sand. As the dunes slowly become larger and more stable so the variety of plants increases, encouraged by the accumulation of organic matter and the leaching out of the salt. The older, fixed dunes with extensive plant cover are sometimes called 'grey' dunes because of the colour of the lichens and mosses they support. Clumps of marram grass are favourite nesting sites for the meadow pipit.

Cley Windmill

The brick-built tower windmill at Cley-Next-the-Sea – overlooking Blakeney Harbour, the River Glaven and the Cley Marshes nature reserve – is a prominent landmark on the North Norfolk coast. Built in the early eighteenth century, it ceased working in *c.* 1912 and was subsequently converted into a private residence. Since 1983 it has been run as a guest house. During medieval times, the Glaven was navigable as far inland as Glandford: with the ports of Cley and Wiveton, centred around their respective churches, facing each other across a wide expanse of tidal water. The haven slowly began to silt up in the early seventeenth century, due to the construction of flood-protection and land-reclamation banks. The building of a new quay nearer the sea, shifted the centre of Cley north, to the area where the windmill now stands. Although Cley's importance as a port declined, trade did not finally cease until 1884, when the railway came to Holt, a few miles to the south-east. The distant tower in the photograph belongs to Blakeney church.

NORWICH AND THE BROADS

Unlike windmills, which were built for grinding corn into flour, windpumps were designed to keep the marshes, or 'levels', drained by lifting water up into the rivers and dykes. On the banks of the River Ant at How Hill, where there is a 353-acre traditionally managed nature reserve, are three drainage mills – all structurally different. The Turf Fen windpump has a brick tower, topped by a typical Norfolk boat-shaped cap. On the opposite bank of the river is an open-framed timber trestle pump, named after the Boardman family of How Hill House. Built in 1912, its scoop-wheel has now been replaced by a turbine pump. Clayrack Mill, nearby, is a working hollow post windpump with its original scoop-wheel intact. Moved from Ranworth marshes where it was erected in the mid nineteenth century, it was reconstructed on the present site in 1981. Toad Hole Cottage, built in 1728 and later extended slightly, has been furnished much as it would have been when it was lived in by a Victorian marshman and his family.

After receiving the waters of the River Wensum near Norwich – the ancient capital of Norfolk – the Yare meanders gently in an easterly direction through the Broads to enter the North Sea at the town of Great Yarmouth. Although the tidal Broadland waterway network is navigable right up to Norwich, the cathedral city ceased to be an inland port of consequence in the early twentieth century.

During medieval times, the city of Norwich was one of the richest in England, its prosperity based primarily on the export of wool and cloth to continental Europe. Dominated by the great stone keep of the Norman castle, Norwich was protected on its eastern side by the sweeping double bend of the Wensum and, on its western and northern sides, by defensive earthworks (reinforced by walls, mainly composed of flint, built between 1297 and 1334). The entrances to the city by road were also fortified. Traffic entering or leaving by way of the river was controlled by a chain, or 'boom', slung between two towers, one on either side of the Wensum. Today, the passage upstream to the dock and warehouse district is kept open by two moving bridges – one a swing bridge and the other a counterbalanced lift bridge.

Before 1833, when work was completed on the 'New Cut' (a two-and-a-half-mile-long canal linking Reedham on the Yare to Haddiscoe on the Waveney), cargoes bound for Norwich had to be transferred from deep-hulled sea-going to shallow-draught river vessels at Yarmouth, and vice versa for goods heading the other way. Although the arrangement brought enormous benefits to Yarmouth, Norwich increasingly resented having to pay tolls on all merchandise passing through the seaport.

Not surprisingly, when the burgesses of Yarmouth learned of the proposal to make Norwich a port in its own right (by giving it direct access to the sea at Yarmouth), they did everything in their power to prevent this happening. Norwich countered their efforts by submitting an alternative proposal – the building of 'New Cut', which would open a route from the city to the sea by way of Oulton Broad and Lowestoft, thereby avoiding Yarmouth altogether. In spite of fierce opposition from Yarmouth, Parliament authorized the construction of the canal and work commenced in 1827. The 'New Cut' had only been in operation for about 15 years when it was made virtually redundant by improvements to the navigation of the lower Yare and Breydon Water, making it possible, at last, for ships from Norwich to enter the sea at Yarmouth. By then, however, the construction of the railway line between Norwich and Yarmouth had been completed, shortly followed by the building of the railway line to Lowestoft.

Before the development of a reliable road and rail network, which came into being during the eighteenth and nineteenth centuries, the rivers and lakes of the Broads were the main transport routes for both passengers and cargo. Although the clinker-built keel, with its central mast and single square sail, was one of the earliest kinds of sailing craft to operate on the Broads, it was the Norfolk wherry (a type of half-decked commercial boat, such as a barge) that dominated the waterways from the late sixteenth century onwards. Specially designed to sail the shallow, narrow and winding rivers of the Broads, the wherry is said to owe its development to the arrival of Dutch refugees, who introduced the stepped-forward mast and distinctive gaff sail. This fore-and-aft rig enabled the wherries to sail into, or much closer to the wind and, therefore, make faster progress against headwinds. It also improved the craft's manoeuvrability, thus making it relatively simple – when shooting low bridges, for example – for one person quickly to lower and raise both mast and sail. From being able to carry about five tons, the wherries (crewed usually by two people – often the wherryman and his wife) gradually increased in size, strength and capacity until they reached the potential for carrying about 40 tons of cargo. The largest wherry, the *Wonder*, weighed about 80 tons when fully laden. Because of the difference in salinity, and therefore buoyancy, between seawater and freshwater, a shallow-draught wherry loaded 'down to the bins', or gunwales, in Yarmouth would often have water lapping over its deck by the time it arrived at the quay in Norwich. Most wherries were clinker-built of oak, but a few were built of steel.

After the growth in popularity of the Broads as a holiday centre in the mid nineteenth century, enterprising wherrymen started to carry holidaymakers in their craft during the summer months. Inevitably, by the late 1880s, boat-builders sensitive to this development were starting to produce custom-designed 'pleasure wherries', and later saw the introduction of 'wherry yachts'. As trading vessels declined on the Broads because of improved road and rail transport, so the number of holiday boats and cruisers increased. Estimates suggest that on the waterways today there are more than 12,000 boats carrying in total about three-quarters of a million people a year.

Some two thousand years ago, the Broads formed part of a vast and complex estuary, known to the Romans as *Gariensis Ostium*, the principal mouth of which stretched between the higher ground now occupied by Caister-on-Sea in the north and Burgh Castle in the south, and reached inland for several miles up the valleys of the Bure, Ant, Waveney and Yare. The latter river, in fact, led to Caistor St Edmund (the Roman city of

Venta Icenorum), three miles south of Norwich. The gradual formation of a shingle spit and sand bank from Caister eventually blocked the mouth of the main estuary, thus diverting the waters of the Yare southward. During Anglo-Saxon times, the estuarial outlets steadily silted up and, by the time of the Norman Conquest in 1066, the fishing settlement, that was to develop into Great Yarmouth, had been established on the spit. Today, all the waters of the Broads either empty into the sea at Yarmouth or at Lowestoft. It was initially thought that the Broads – a series of shallow lakes, or meres – were of natural origin. In the 1950s, however, comprehensive research material gathered from various sources, including monastic records, proved that they are in fact the flooded remains of shallow peat diggings that were created in medieval times and then later permanently flooded. The accounts of Norwich Cathedral Priory, for example, show that in the early fourteenth century up to 400,000 turves were purchased for heating and cooking in a single year. The use of massive quantities of peat for fuel (and for extracting salt from seawater) was essentially one of demand for, during the Middle Ages, eastern Norfolk was one of the most populous areas in all of Britain. Another factor leading to the extraction of large quantities of peat was that since most of the original forest had been cleared for farming, wood, as an alternative source of fuel, was in short supply.

Since the digging of peat was abandoned because of rising water levels in the late thirteenth and fourteenth centuries, the Broads have gradually been deteriorating due to the accumulation of river-borne mud. The area of open water that existed in the mid nineteenth century was more than double what it is today. Given the pollution caused by sewage and agricultural effluent in recent times, and added to this the damage brought about by heavy boat traffic, it is not surprising that much of the water has turned murky and the rich diversity of plant and animal life has been drastically reduced. Obviously, there is no simple solution to the problems of the Broads. However, without the traditional forms of countryside management, open water would develop through fen to 'carr' and, eventually, oak woodland. It is imperative, therefore, that this unique wetland habitat is maintained and the quality of its water improved, thereby encouraging the aquatic vegetation and wildlife to return once more. A start has already been made. The classic example being Cockshoot Broad, which has been brought back to life and revitalized through isolation and dredging.

In 1989, the Broads, which cover an area of some 117 square miles and contain 40 or so meres, were designated a National Park. For many boating enthusiasts the journey through some 125 miles of lock-free navigations leads inevitably to Norwich – where shipping links with Yarmouth have been maintained and, seemingly, old antagonisms have been forgotten.

St Olave's Priory

Situated near an ancient ferry across the River Waveney, six miles south-west of Great Yarmouth, St Olave's priory was founded for Augustinian canons by Robert Fitz Osbert in c. 1216. Like the village, the monastery derives its name from Olaf, the king and patron saint of Norway, who was killed in battle in 1030. At its dissolution in 1537, the priory (never a large or wealthy house) contained only six canons, including the prior. Some of the buildings, including most of the church, were subsequently pulled down and the materials used in the construction of the house close by. The refectory undercroft, built in c. 1300, is an important example of the early use of brick vaulting. One of the five columns of Purbeck marble, which carry the vaulted ceiling, stands on a Roman millstone. The priory remains are now in the care of English Heritage. St Olave's windpump (or Priory Mill) is one of several drainage mills in the area. Herringfleet Mill, just across the Norfolk border into Suffolk, is the only timber-built smock windpump to survive in the Broads.

Berney Arms Windmill, *from Burgh Castle*

Isolated amid extensive re-claimed marshland on the west bank of the River Yare, just before it flows into Breydon Water, the seven-storey, 70-feet-high Berney Arms High Mill is the tallest windpump in England. Although a prominent landmark for miles around, the black-tarred tower mill, with its large encased scoop-wheel, is difficult to reach on foot. The easiest approach is by river, though trains do occasionally stop at the Berney Arms Station (about half a mile distant). Before its conversion into a water pump, the nineteenth-century mill was used to grind cement clinker. Now in the care of English Heritage, it houses an exhibition on wind-mills. The nearby Berney Arms Inn, despite its remoteness, is popular during the summer season. Before the land was drained and used as summer grazing pasture for cattle, sheep and horses, the area (part of the Halvergate Marshes) was a vast tidal estuary of mudflats and saltmarshes. Although changes in farming practices since the Second World War threatened to destroy the unique marsh landscape, it is now protected.

Burgh Castle

Overlooking Breydon Water and the flat expanses of the Halvergate Marshes – almost four miles south-west of Great Yarmouth – Burgh Castle (or *Gariannonum*) was built by the Romans in the late third century to defend the east coast from raids by Saxon pirates. One of a chain of defensive garrisons, known as the 'Saxon Shore' forts, it originally guarded a harbour at the mouth of a wide and navigable river estuary. On the opposite and northern side of the water, incidentally, stood the Roman port and town of Caister, while the land now occupied by Great Yarmouth lay submerged beneath the sea. The massive walls, standing almost to their full height, are built of rubble concrete, with alternating courses of bricks and flints. Tradition says that the site was given to St Fursey in the seventh century by Sigeberht, King of the East Angles, for the foundation of a monastery. After the Conquest, the Normans converted the fort into a motte-and-bailey castle. The motte, however, was destroyed in 1839.

Lower Close,
Norwich

In 1094, after the see of East Anglia was moved from Thetford to Norwich, Bishop Herbert de Losinga began work on the creation of the priory precinct, and, two years later, he laid the foundation stone of the cathedral (completed in c. 1145, some 26 years after his death). Despite the fact that the Norman cathedral and priory brought great wealth to the city, the inhabitants bitterly resented the loss of the eastern side of the Anglo-Saxon town, especially the destruction of St Michael's church and part of Tombland. The dispute over who held the market rights in Tombland – the monks or the townspeople – came to a head in 1272, when the citizens broke down the precinct gates, stormed into the Close, burned down many of the wooden priory buildings, including the church of St Ethelbert, and severely damaged the cathedral. The spire was blown down during a gale in 1362, struck by lightning in 1463 and rebuilt in its present form in 1480. Many of the houses in the Upper and Lower Close – which runs down to the River Wensum – originated as monastic buildings.

St Benet's Abbey,
near Horning

Standing on the north bank of the River Bure, between its junctions with the Ant and Thurne, are the striking remains of St Benet's Abbey, first founded in the ninth century and refounded by King Canute in c. 1020. Although the Benedictine abbey was abandoned in 1545, it is remarkable for being the only religious house in England that was not dissolved by Henry VIII. Uniquely, in 1536 the king not only appointed the last abbot, William Reppes (or Rugge), Bishop of Norwich, he also combined the bishopric with the abbacy. Today, as the Abbot of St Benet's, the Bishop of Norwich visits the ruins of the abbey church once a year on the first Sunday in August to hold a service. The large oak cross, erected in 1987 to mark the position of the High Altar, came from the Royal Estate at Sandringham. In the eighteenth century, a brick tower windpump (now derelict) was erected within the ruins of the monastic gatehouse. Although essentially a drainage mill, it may also have been used to extract oil from colza seeds for lamps.

Wymondham Abbey

The two tall towers of Wymondham abbey church dominate the countryside for miles around. Standing at opposite ends of the Romanesque nave, the towers represent well over 300 years of animosity between the monks and the townspeople. The quarrels started with the foundation of the Benedictine priory by William de Albini in 1107. Although the founder stipulated that part of the priory church should serve as the parish church, the details were ambiguous. In 1249, in an unsuccessful attempt to resolve the long-standing dispute, Pope Innocent IV ruled that the town should have the nave, north aisle and north-west tower, and the monks the rest. When the monks replaced the Norman central tower with the present octagonal bell tower, completed in 1409, they also erected a solid wall across the nave. Further strife, which included the townspeople petitioning Henry IV, led to the parishioners building the even-higher (but unfinished) west tower in 1447. The priory became an abbey in 1448, less than a century before its dissolution by Henry VIII.

Village Green,
Woodbastwick

With its thatched-and-tiled cottages, flint church and pumphouse on the village green, Woodbastwick is part of a Broadland estate owned by the Cator family since the early nineteenth century. The thatched church of St Fabian and St Sebastian, restored by George Gilbert Scott in 1878, dates from the late thirteenth or the early fourteenth century. Its dedication is considered to be unique in England. The village sign, depicting a man tying up his leggings with 'bast' (the pliable inner bark of lime trees), suggests that 'Woodbastwick' means 'the wooded place where bast can be found'. In 1949, Colonel Cator gave both Ranworth and Cockshoot Broads to the Norfolk Naturalists Trust. They now form part of the Bure Marshes National Nature Reserve. The floating timber-and-thatched Broadland Conservation Centre at Ranworth was opened in 1976. Cockshoot Broad, badly silted up and almost devoid of wildlife, has been dramatically restored by a project completed in 1982, which involved isolating it from the River Bure by a dam and suction dredging some 40,000 cubic yards of mud.

Hickling Broad

The largest of the broads covering 1,360 acres, Hickling Broad is a National Nature Reserve, managed by the Norfolk Naturalists Trust in conjunction with the Nature Conservancy Council. Among its rich diversity of habitats are reed and sedge beds, grazing marshes, fen woodland, drainage ditches, shallow ponds and 300 acres of open, slightly salty water. These, in turn, attract a great variety of plants and wildlife, including such rarities as the holly leaved naiad, swallowtail butterfly and Norfolk hawker dragonfly. The reserve is also an important breeding site for bittern, marsh harrier, bearded reedling and water rail. In order to improve the quality of water in the broad and to preserve the ever-changing character of the wetland environment, local farmers are encouraged to limit the use of chemicals, maintain high water levels in the dykes, and not convert grazing land to arable. The reed and sedge beds are regularly harvested for thatch. Other features on the reserve include a visitor centre, nature trails and observation hides.

St Margaret's Church,
Antingham

Three miles north-west of North Walsham, Antingham is one of at least 12 villages in Norfolk having two medieval parish churches in the same churchyard. The ivy-covered ruin of St Margaret's dates from the early twelfth century. The tower was added to the nave in the early fourteenth century, while the chancel was built in the fourteenth or fifteenth century. By the end of the seventeenth century, the village was too small to support two churches and St Margaret's was abandoned. St Mary's, built in the Decorated style between c. 1330 and 1360, contains a thirteenth-century Purbeck marble font, which may have originally belonged to St Margaret's. The painted Pre-Raphaelite glass in the south chancel window, dating from 1865, is by Morris and Company. A memorial brass to Richard Calthorpe, who died in 1554, shows him in full armour with 19 of his children in mourning. Barge Farm serves as a reminder that Antingham was once connected to Dilham and the Broads network of waterways by a ten-mile-long canal, which was opened in 1826.

Pull's Ferry,
Norwich

In the late eleventh century, before work began on building the cathedral and priory at Norwich, a short and narrow canal was dug to enable boats to carry materials right up to the site of construction: Caen stone from Normandy, iron from Sweden and timber from the shores of the Baltic Sea. Having transferred the materials from sea-going ships to river-vessels at Great Yarmouth, they were transported inland up the Yare and Wensum to Norwich. After the priory had been completed, the canal – linking the Wensum to the Cathedral Close – proved to be an invaluable asset, and for hundreds of years it was used to bring bulky goods (such as peat from the Broads) into the heart of the monastic precinct. The watergate (shown in the photograph) was built in the fifteenth century to guard the river entrance to the canal. While, beside it, the ferryman's house – Pull's Ferry – was erected shortly after the priory's dissolution in 1538. Named after the nineteenth-century ferryman, John Pull, the house was also used as an inn. The ferry service ceased in the 1930s.

St Nicholas's Church,
Great Yarmouth

About 2,000 years ago the land now occupied by Great Yarmouth and the parish church of St Nicholas (the largest in Norfolk) did not exist. It lay submerged at the mouth of a vast estuary that led inland to Caistor St Edmund, near Norwich, where the Romans established their regional capital, *Venta Icenorum*. The gradual formation of a sand bank eventually blocked the passage of the River Yare to the sea and diverted its course southwards. Although a thriving town was recorded on the sandbank in the Domesday survey of 1086, Yarmouth may still have been an island in the thirteenth century. Sand, however, constantly blocked the harbour entrance and the townspeople were forced to cut new channels to keep the port (facing the river, not the sea) open to shipping. Six times, between 1347 and 1549, they created an artificial mouth through which the Yare could enter the sea, and each time it silted up. The present Yare mouth, at Gorleston-on-Sea, has been in existence since 1614. Today, the historic port, noted for its herring fleet, is a large and popular holiday resort.

Parish Church,
North Walsham

The 'wool' church of St Nicholas (formerly dedicated to the Blessed Virgin Mary) at North Walsham seems to have had more than its fair share of ill fortune. Rebuilding, which began in c. 1330 on the site of an Anglo-Saxon foundation, was interrupted by the Black Death in 1348, 1361 and 1369. The drastic reduction in the population, including skilled craftsmen, led to a simplification in the design of most of the windows. A further delay occurred during the Peasants' Revolt of 1381, when several thousand labourers sought sanctuary inside the church after being defeated in a battle outside the town by Henry le Despencer, Bishop of Norwich. Showing no respect for the building or the right of sanctuary, the bishop instantly slaughtered all who were captured. On 16 May 1724, the day after the bells had been rung for many hours to celebrate the town's 'Ascension Day Fayre', the tower – originally 147 feet high and topped by a 23-feet spire – partly collapsed. It has not been rebuilt. The church is the second largest in Norfolk.

Elm Hill,
Norwich

Within the boundaries of Norwich's medieval defences are many ancient streets with buildings dating from the sixteenth and seventeenth centuries. One of the best known is the winding Elm Hill, located east of the cathedral, and beyond Tombland (the city's earliest marketplace). Among the houses on the north side of the street is the Elizabethan 'Strangers' Club' (like 'Strangers' Hall', further east, it may have been named after Dutch refugees, or 'Strangers', who settled in the town); while on the south side is the house of Thomas Pettus, sheriff in 1566 and mayor in 1590. The Briton's Arms, the half-timbered coffee-house overlooking the cobbled, tree-shaded square, was formerly an inn. Traditionally, Norwich is said to have had an inn for every day of the year, and a church for every Sunday. Although redundant, the church of St Simon and St Jude, at the bottom of the hill in Wensum Street, is one of more than 30 medieval parish churches to survive in the inner city. St Peter Hungate Church, at the top of Elm Street, which was built in 1460, is now used as a museum.

Horsey Windpump

Just south of the compact, tree-shaded village of Horsey, with its ancient church and nineteenth-century Hall, Horsey windpump was built to lift water into the Broads from the surrounding low-lying fields by way of the entirely artificial Horsey Staithe. However, despite being less than two miles from the coast, the water has to travel more than 20 miles by way of the rivers Thurne and Bure before reaching the sea at Great Yarmouth. When the four-storey drainage pump was converted to steam, coal was brought to the staithe (a landing-place for boats) by wherry. Today, as well as providing moorings for pleasure craft, the staithe is used as a road-transport collection point for harvested bundles of reed and sedge brought by boat. The pump, together with Horsey Hall, Horsey Mere and the adjoining marshes, marrams and farmland was acquired by the National Trust in 1948. Despite the presence of a sea-bank, the area has not escaped serious flooding. In 1938 and 1953, for example, thousands of acres were inundated. Seepage from the sea has resulted in the Mere being slightly salty.

Thurne Dyke Windpump,
Thurne

Near the Broadland village of
Thurne are two restored drainage
windpumps of the brick tower
type, with white caps and sails.
Standing in close proximity to
one another on opposite banks of
the River Thurne, not far from
its junction with the Bure at
Thurne Mouth, the white-
painted, timber-clad windpump
is named after the Thurne Dyke,
while the red-brick mill is named
after St Benet's Level. The former contains a small exhibition
of Broadland windpumps: the
latter, however, is not open to
the public. Thurne village, with
its thatched church, general store
and The Lion Inn, stands at the
eastern end of the Thurne Dyke.
Dating from the thirteenth century, the parish church of St
Edmund, with its embattled west
tower, is a prominent Broadland
landmark. St Benet's Abbey –
two miles away across the flat,
almost treeless grazing marshes –
can be seen through a squint in
the base of the tower. Tradition
says that a lantern placed in the
peephole was used to send sig-
nals to the monks.

Marram Hills,
Waxham

Although much of the low-lying
stretch of coast between
Winterton-on-Sea and Happisburgh is protected by a sea wall
– capped by sand dunes and stabilized by plants with binding
roots, such as marram grass – the
area has suffered from serious
flooding over the centuries. A
storm in November 1897
breached the wall at Horsey and
caused much damage. After a
further breach in February 1938,
which inundated 15 square miles
between Sea Palling and Winterton (reaching as far inland as
Potter Heigham and causing
seawater to enter the Broadland
waterway network with disastrous consequences for plant
and animal life), the wall was
substantially strengthened.
Nevertheless, the sea broke
through again in early 1953,
prompting the construction of
additional defensive embankments. Since then, the heights of
the dunes have risen, but further
flooding remains an ever-present
threat. For many old villages,
however, coastal defences have
come too late. Waxham, for
example, was once two villages.
Only Great Waxham, with its
church, walled manor and Great
Barn, survives.

Happisburgh Lighthouse

In 1722-3 Daniel Defoe travelled northward along the Norfolk coast from Great Yarmouth to Cromer and, despite knowing that the stretch was 'one of the most dangerous and most fatal to the sailors in *all* England', was surprised to find that 'the farmers, and country people had scarce a barn, or a shed, or a stable; nay, not the pales of their yards, and gardens, not a hogsty, not a necessary-house, but what was built of old planks, beams, wales and timbers, & c. the wrecks of ships, and ruins of mariners' and merchants' fortunes.' In 1692, by way of a 'melancholy example', he added in *A Tour Thro' the Whole Island of Great Britain*, that 'above 200 sail of ships, and above a thousand people perished in . . .one miserable night, very few escaping.' Considering the dangers to shipping, especially from offshore sandbanks, warning beacons were essential. Before a lighthouse was built at Happisburgh, the 110-feet-high church tower served as a landmark. The present lighthouse was erected in 1791. A second light, in danger of collapse from cliff erosion, was demolished in 1883.

Sea Defences,
Sea Palling

Like many settlements along the Norfolk coast, Sea Palling has been fighting an unremitting battle for survival against coastal erosion and inundation by the sea for centuries. Although it escaped relatively unscathed from the floods of 1938, the village suffered severe damage when the sea burst through its defensive wall of dunes in 1953. In 1994 – after detailed studies on the risk to East Anglia from rising seas and sinking coastlines (caused by Britain tilting geologically on a north-south axis to the east) – the National Rivers Authority launched a massive coastal defence programme, starting with the offshore construction of four walls, or 'reefs', made with large granite blocks, just north of Sea Palling. Eventually there will be 16 shore-parallel reefs stretching between Winterton and Happisburgh. But whether they will be enough to prevent further flooding to a coast prone to the dangerous combination of winds and tides, known as the North Sea surge, only time will tell. To try to protect the entire eastern coast, however, would be unrealistic.

BURY ST EDMUNDS AND SUFFOLK

Framlingham Castle

Occupying the site of an earlier fortress, built by Roger Bigod I in *c.* 1100 and destroyed by Henry II in 1175-7, Framlingham Castle is an early example of the style of stronghold that relied heavily on a massive curtain wall with flanking towers for its main defence, rather than the traditional Norman design of keep and bailey. From the exterior it appears almost the same as when it was built by Roger Bigod II, 2nd Earl of Norfolk, in *c.* 1190. The buildings within the walls, however, are a mixture of historical styles, reflecting the castle's changing roles as a fortress, an Elizabeth prison for recusant priests (those who refused to accept the new Church of England) and a seventeenth- and eighteenth-century poor house (initially only for children). It also served as a county court, drill hall and fire station before being placed in the care of the State in 1913. Near the castle, the parish church of St Michael contains a magnificent collection of monuments to the Howards, Dukes of Norfolk, who made Framlingham their principal residence in the late fifteenth century.

After the body of Edmund, King of the East Angles, was enshrined at *Bedericsworth* (Bury) in *c.* 903, the monastery became a leading centre of pilgrimage and, ultimately, one of the richest and most powerful Benedictine houses in all of England. In honour of the 'Shrine of a King', the thriving medieval market town, which grew up beside the abbey after the Norman Conquest, changed its name to Bury St Edmunds, or St Edmundsbury. It was at St Edmund's altar in the abbey church on 20 November 1214 that the barons gathered to swear to go to war against King John unless he accepted the demands that eventually formed the basis of the historic Magna Carta.

Today, a statue of the saint and martyr, by the Suffolk-born sculptor Elisabeth Frink, stands on the green between the cathedral, the Norman Tower and the remains of the west front of the abbey. Very little is known with any certainty about the life of Edmund, but not long after his death he came to be revered as a martyr and was the subject of many popular legends.

According to tradition, the saint was born in Nuremberg, Germany and, while he was still a youth, was chosen by God to become the King of the East Angles. In 855, after crossing the sea from Germany, he landed at Hunstanton in Norfolk to claim his kingdom. Almost at the very spot where he knelt down to pray and ask God's blessing for himself and his people, a spring of healing water gushed forth from the ground. He was crowned on Christmas Day, possibly at Bures in Suffolk (then a royal capital), and, despite his tender age, he apparently ruled well and wisely, devoting himself to securing peace and happiness for all of his subjects.

Edmund had reigned for only 14 years when he was killed by the invading Danish army, under the command of Ivar the Boneless, which overran East Anglia in 869. Although some people maintain that he died in battle, others suggest that he surrendered to the Danes in the hope that they would leave his people in peace. Had he renounced his Christian faith, his life may have been spared by the Danes. Rather than take this option, he refused and was subsequently tied to a tree and his body shot full of arrows. His head was then hacked off and thrown into a nearby wood, where a wolf stood guard over it until it was retrieved and miraculously rejoined to his body. Because the holy king died at the hands of the Danes, it has also been suggested that he was 'blood-eagled' as a sacrificial offering to the Scandinavian god Odin. A tenth-century account of Edmund's life states that he died at a place called Haeglesidun, which has been variously identified with Hoxne in Suffolk or Hellesdon in Norfolk. Recent research, however, favours a field known as Hellesdon at Bradfield St Clare, which is south-east of Bury St Edmunds. A series of medieval paintings, depicting various scenes from the life of St Edmund, can be found on the north wall of the nave in the parish church at Thornham Parva, which, incidentally, is only six miles from a monument marking the saint's alleged place of execution at Hoxne.

It was while he was searching with a metal detector for a friend's lost hammer in a field at Hoxne, in 1992, that Eric Lawes discovered a valuable hoard of Roman treasure. Subsequent excavation of the site by professional archaeologists brought to light nearly 15,000 gold, silver and bronze coins, the oldest ones dating from AD 337-40. As well as the coins, the archaeologists also discovered some 200 other items, including jewellery and tableware. However, unlike the late-Roman treasure unearthed at Gallows Hill, Thetford, in 1979, which had pagan religious dedications, the Hoxne treasure contained inscriptions that were entirely Christian in origin.

Although there have been other discoveries of ancient hordes of treasure buried in the soil of East Anglia – notably at Mildenhall, Snettisham and Ipswich – the hoard unearthed at Sutton Hoo, situated near Woodbridge, in 1939, proved to be the richest ever found anywhere in Britain. Excavation of a large mound – one of a group of barrows overlooking the River Deben – revealed the tomb of an Anglo-Saxon king, thought possibly to be Raedwald (who died in about 625). He was buried in a huge wooden ship, which measured nearly 90 feet in length, together with a fabulous collection of goods, including a magnificent ceremonial helmet. No human remains were found, however, despite the fact that the goods inside the grave had lain undisturbed there for more than thirteen centuries. It now appears that Sutton Hoo was the royal burial ground for the powerful dynasty of East Anglian kings, founded by Wuffa, whose palace stood at Rendlesham, some four miles upstream.

Among the wealth of folklore and legends that abound in East Anglia – a region that was gripped by witch-hunting hysteria during the sixteenth and seventeenth centuries – is a tradition that three holy crowns were buried around the coastline to protect England from the peril of foreign invasion. If, as has been suggested, one belonged to Sigeberht, son of Raedwald, then presumably they were hidden not in Anglo-Saxon times, but sometime after the Norman Conquest. One crown is believed to have been lost when Dunwich crumbled into the sea. Another, dug up at Rendlesham in the eighteenth century, was apparently melted down for its silver content and, therefore, lost forever. While the third – like King John's treasure – has yet to be found. In addition to ghosts, fairies, giants and fabulous beasts of various descriptions, the eastern counties have long been haunted by a lone spectral hound, said to have huge, red, saucer-shaped eyes, known as Black or Old Shuck. Although the hound is often described as being a demon and a harbinger of death, in some parts of the region he is regarded in a much different light – as a friendly omen that has even been known to protect and guide lonely travellers in danger. Sometimes he is invisible, giving his presence away only by his hot and sulphurous breath, his blood-curdling howls or the padding of his monstrous paws. Legend has it that he is also able to take on human form, as happened at Lowestoft when Old Shuck appeared as a dark-complexioned stranger and attempted to lure a fisher boy to certain death out at sea. Fortunately, the boy was rescued by a passing ship, but not before he had been badly savaged around the neck.

What with the recorded capture of a wild and hairy 'merman' at Orford in the late twelfth century, as well as the alleged landing of an Unidentified Flying Object (UFO) near two RAF NATO bases in Rendlesham Forest in 1980, Suffolk seems to attract more than its fair share of strange and unearthly visitors. At Woolpit, about seven miles east of Bury St Edmunds, the twelfth-century chronicler William of Newburgh, reported the sudden and mysterious appearance of two green-skinned children – one a boy and the other a girl – who were dressed in clothes of a strange colour and made of unfamiliar materials. They also spoke an entirely unknown language. Although the boy died shortly after his baptism, the girl continued in good health and, as she gradually grew accustomed to eating the same food as the villagers, so her skin turned to a more natural colour. She eventually learned to speak English and then married a man hailing from King's Lynn. When she was asked to explain how she and the boy had come to be in Woolpit, she said that they were inhabitants of the land of St Martin and, while following their father's flocks, they were somehow entranced by the sound of bells. The next thing she claimed to have remembered was standing in the fields among the reapers at Woolpit. In another account, the children emerged out of a pit used for trapping wolves (from which the village derived its name).

Numerous representations of the wolf that guarded the head of St Edmund, severed by the invading Danes, can be found in and around Bury St Edmunds, including a carving on the Bishop's Throne in the cathedral. During the reign of King John, the relics of the saint were reputedly stolen and taken to Toulouse Abbey in France. Although the present whereabouts and authenticity of his remains are disputed, the focus of the king and martyr's cult remains at Bury St Edmunds – where, for more than a thousand years, the legends have far outweighed the facts.

'Little Hall',
Lavenham

Situated on an eminence above the valley of the Brad, the medieval market town of Lavenham is noted for its streets lined with timber-framed houses, many, like 'Little Hall', supporting overhanging jetties. Its development as a cloth-making centre – famed for its blue broadcloth – stemmed from the 1330s when Edward III encouraged Flemish weavers to settle in England. The growing prosperity of the town in the fifteenth century is reflected in many of its buildings. Above all, in the magnificent 'wool' church of St Peter and St Paul, rebuilt in the Late Perpendicular style with money from wealthy clothiers, and by the lord of the manor, John de Vere, 13th Earl of Oxford. Many of the houses and cottages were plastered over in the late seventeenth century, and, in some cases, decoration was added in the form of pargeting. The following century, the fronts and overhangs of some of the properties were hidden behind a façade of Georgian brick. Today the trend is to re-expose the timber-framing, which, traditionally in Suffolk, is vertical close studding.

Moot Hall,
Aldeburgh

Built in the mid sixteenth century, when Aldeburgh was a fishing and ship-building port of some importance, the timber-framed Moot Hall – now housing a museum of the town's history – was originally open at the north end of the ground floor for market trading. It once stood two rows of houses back from the sea, but coastal erosion has now placed it almost on the shingle beach. Aldeburgh is probably most famous for being the birthplace of the poet George Crabbe (1754-1832), and the home of the composer Benjamin Britten (1913-76). Britten's opera *Peter Grimes* (1945) was inspired by one of the tales in Crabbe's Aldeburgh poem *The Borough* (1810). In 1948, Britten co-founded the town's annual music festival, held in June. Since 1967, however, the major performances have been staged in the Maltings concert hall, five miles inland at Snape. The hall had to be completely restored after the malthouse was gutted by fire in 1969. It was from here that malt, made from Suffolk barley, was once shipped down the River Alde to breweries in London and Norwich.

Orford Castle

Distinguished by the fact that it is the earliest castle in Britain for which there are detailed records of construction and costs, Orford was begun in 1165 and completed in 1173 at a total cost of £1,413 9s 2d (about a seventh of the annual total basic revenues of the Crown). Originally commissioned by Henry II as a royal stronghold and coastal defence, it is also noted for the unusual design of the keep – finished in just two years from 1165, and all that now survives of the castle above ground. Instead of the characteristic great rectangular tower of the period, the external walls of the keep are polygonal in plan, with three huge rectangular turrets acting as buttresses. According to the thirteenth-century chronicler Ralph of Coggeshall, local fishermen caught a naked hairy creature 'like a man in all his members' and handed him over to the first constable of the castle, Bartholomew de Glanville. Known as the Wild Man of Orford, the 'merman' eventually escaped and returned to the sea.

Holy Trinity Church, *Long Melford*

Situated on the Chad Brook, near its confluence with the Stour, Long Melford's history dates back to Roman times when the river was navigable. Its long main street – with Holy Trinity church at one end and Melford Place at the other – follows the line of an old Roman road. Before the Dissolution, the manor belonged to Bury St Edmunds abbey. The estate was subsequently granted to Sir William Cordell, builder of Melford Hall (now owned by the National Trust). In 1578, three years before his death, Cordell entertained Elizabeth I at the house. His magnificent tomb stands in front of the high altar of the 'wool' church. Nearby is the tomb of John Clopton, a wealthy cloth merchant and the principal founder of the church, which was completed in 1484 (the Lady Chapel and Clopton Chantry Chapel were added a few years later). Lightning destroyed the original church tower in *c.* 1710 and, although rebuilt, it was replaced in 1903. The Martyns, also great benefactors of the church, lived at Melford Place from the fifteenth to the eighteenth centuries.

Ickworth House

Located in the village of Horringer, three miles south-west of Bury St Edmunds, Ickworth House was begun in 1795 by the 4th Earl of Bristol and Bishop of Derry, Frederick Augustus Hervey. Work ceased when the Earl-Bishop died in Italy in 1803. The house was completed 26 years later by his son, Frederick Hervey, the 5th Earl (created 1st Marquess of Bristol in 1826). It was his father's intention to live in the oval rotunda – inspired by John Plaw's Belle Isle round house on Lake Windermere – and to use the long curved wings to house his art collections. The 5th Earl, however, turned the east wing into living quarters and the rotunda, with its great Entrance Hall and lofty state rooms, into a place for entertaining and a setting for the family treasures. The west wing was left uncompleted. Later alterations included the decoration of the Pompeiian Room by JD Crace in 1879 and the remodelling of the east wing by Reginald Blomfield in 1907-9. The house, set in 'Capability' Brown parkland, is now owned by the National Trust.

Martello Tower,
Aldeburgh

In the late eighteenth and early nineteenth centuries, when England was at war with France, the British Government decided to strengthen its coastal defences against a possible Napoleonic invasion. Between 1805 and 1812, a chain of 103 bomb-proof gun towers were erected around the coast from Slaughden, near Aldeburgh, to Seaford in Sussex. Ironically, the idea for the small forts – most of which resemble upturned flower pots – came from a tower on the island of Corsica, Napoleon's birthplace. Its location at Mortella Point gave rise to the name 'Martello' tower. The tower at Slaughden is not only the northernmost of the chain, it is quatrefoil in design and, therefore, completely different to all the others. Now owned by the Landmark Trust, it has been restored and converted into holiday accommodation. The River Alde, which flows past the tower, is diverted south by a shingle bank, runs roughly parallel to the coast for some ten miles, changes its name to the River Ore, and finally enters the sea near Hollesley.

High Street, Lavenham

Although its origins date back at least to Anglo-Saxon times, Lavenham reached the height of its prosperity in the sixteenth century when – due to a flourishing woollen cloth-making industry – it was the fourteenth richest town in England, richer even than Lincoln and York. Situated at the meeting-point of five highways, the town boasts a wealth of timber-framed houses, most of which were built between 1400 and 1500. Weaving was mainly carried out in cloth-makers' own homes, rather than in purpose-built large-scale premises. Most weavers were dependent on a few rich clothiers, who controlled prices, supplied the raw materials and sold the finished cloth, mainly overseas. Lavenham's famous blue broadcloth was dyed *before* weaving with a preparation obtained from the leaves of woad (*Isatis tinctoria*), hence the expression 'dyed in the wool'. The town's slow and irreversible decline as a cloth-making centre began during the reign of Elizabeth I, when Dutch refugees settled in Colchester bringing with them techniques for producing a wider and cheaper range of fabrics.

'The House in the Clouds', *Thorpeness*

The construction of a planned seaside resort at Thorpeness, two miles north of Aldeburgh, began in 1910 when Glencairn Stuart Ogilvie created The Meare, a 64-acre boating lake fed by the Hundred River. Over the next 20 years, additions to the village complex included a golf course, a boathouse, a country club and a small shopping square. Westbar, the prominent red-brick gatehouse spanning the eastern end of Westgate, conceals a water tower. Another water tower, 85 feet above the ground, has been disguised as a tall house. Built in 1923, the curious structure was originally known as 'Gazebo' or 'gaze about', but is now called 'The House in the Clouds'. At the same time, the windmill, opposite – originally sited at nearby Aldringham and used to grind corn – was converted to pump water up into the 'Clouds'. The arrival of a mains supply in the 1960s, however, made the post mill and both water towers redundant. Today, the windmill is a Heritage Coast centre, while the 'House in the Clouds' is let as holiday accommodation.

West Front, Abbey Church,
Bury St Edmunds

Once one of the greatest and wealthiest Benedictine monasteries in England, the abbey at Bury St Edmunds was dissolved in 1539 and most of its buildings subsequently demolished. All that survives of the magnificent west front of the abbey church of St Edmund, which originally had a soaring central tower with an octagonal tower at each end, is a massive core of flint masonry, denuded of its stone facing and partly buried beneath the ground. During the eighteenth and nineteenth centuries, houses were built into the remains of its three great arches. The base of Abbot Samson's Tower (on the right of the photograph) has been converted into a visitor centre. Facing the west front, the Norman Tower (dating from 1120-48) was designed to be the main gateway to the abbey church as well as a belfry for the nearby church of St James (now St Edmundsbury Cathedral). The Great Gate, north of the Tower, was built to replace the entrance destroyed by the townspeople when they attacked and burned the abbey in 1327.

Melford Hall

The turreted nineteenth-century gatehouse, facing the broad, triangular village green at Long Melford, leads to Melford Hall, a large and impressive red-brick mansion built by William Cordell in the mid sixteenth century. Parts of an earlier building, owned by the Benedictine Abbey of Bury St Edmunds before the Dissolution, may have been incorporated into the structure. Despite later alterations to the house, including the demolition of the eastern or gatehouse wing in the seventeenth century, the exterior – with its tall chimney-stacks and octagonal turrets – remains essentially Elizabethan. Since 1786 the Hall has been the home of the Hyde Parker family and, although it is now in the care of the National Trust, they continue to live there today. Beatrix Potter, the cousin of Ethel, Lady Hyde Parker, was a frequent visitor to the house, staying in the West Bedroom and keeping small animals in the adjoining turret. The Beatrix Potter Room contains some of her sketches and watercolours, including her model of Jemima Puddleduck.

St Edmundsbury Cathedral

Named after the Saxon king and martyr St Edmund, the ancient market and cathedral town of Bury St Edmunds, laid out on a medieval grid plan, lies on the banks of the rivers Linnet and Lark at the meeting-point of seven major roads. The historic importance of the town is encapsulated in its motto: 'Shrine of a King, Cradle of the Law'. The king was St Edmund (d. 869), whose body was brought to the monastery at *Bedericsworth* (Bury) in *c.* 903. It was because of his shrine that the town became one of the major centres of pilgrimage during the early Middle Ages. The latter half of the motto refers to the fact that it was at St Edmund's altar, in 1214, that the barons swore to force King John to accept the demands that became the basis of the Magna Carta. The church of St James, wholly rebuilt in the sixteenth century and much restored by George Gilbert Scott in the 1860s, was given cathedral status in 1914. In 1960-70, under the direction of Stephen Dykes Bower, the building was extended and enlarged. Among the additions were a new choir, crossing, cloister and library.

Blythburgh Church

Overlooking the tidal Angel Marshes, the parish church of the Holy Trinity at Blythburgh dates mainly from the fifteenth century, when increased prosperity from the cloth trade produced a spate of church building in Suffolk. Although noted for its great size, and the spaciousness and simplicity of its interior, the 'Cathedral of the Marshes' bears the scars of certain unwelcome events in its history. The spire, for example, crashed through the roof of the nave during a storm in 1577. According to one report, 'a strange and terrible tempest of lightning' – believed to have been the Devil himself – burst through the wall, 'cleft the door, and returned to the steeple, rent the timber, brake the chains, and fled towards Bungay'. The scorch marks can still be seen on the great north door. Tradition says that the grapeshot holes in the angel roof were caused deliberately by zealous Puritan image-breakers in 1644. It seems, however, that the damage may have been made by over-enthusiastic church-wardens trying to get rid of troublesome birds in the roof.

Gainsborough Statue,
Sudbury

Occupying a prominent position at the top of Market Hill, in front of the redundant church of St Peter at Sudbury, the statue of Thomas Gainsborough (1727-88) – holding palette and brush – was cast in bronze by Bertram Mackennal and unveiled in 1913. Gainsborough, the son of a Nonconformist cloth merchant, was born in the Georgian-fronted house in Gainsborough Street (formerly Sepulchre Street), near the bottom of the hill. It is now a museum and art gallery. At the age of fourteen he left Suffolk to go to London to study art. Shortly after his return to Sudbury in 1748, the artist was commissioned to paint one of his most famous works, *Mr and Mrs Robert Andrews*, in which equal prominence is given to the newly married couple and their country estate of Ballingdon Hall (just south of the wool town). In 1752, Gainsborough set up a studio in Ipswich, seven years later he moved to Bath, and from 1774, until his death, he lived in London. Although he made his living from society portraiture, Gainsborough much preferred to paint landscapes.

St Andrew's Church,
Covehithe

Noted for its church-within-a-church, the lonely hamlet of Covehithe was once a thriving fishing village, until most of the buildings were washed away. Erosion has long been active along this part of the coast, and sometimes it can be extremely severe. In just 24 hours, for example, it has been estimated that the great storm of 1953 removed 300,000 tons of material from the Covehithe cliffs and, in places, the sea encroached as much as 90 feet. Not surprisingly, the lane heading east from the church disappears abruptly at the edge of the cliff. In spite of the fact that the population was never more than 300, the original parish church of St Andrew, built in the fifteenth century, was of cathedral-like proportions. One suspects that it was built more for display – glorification, even – than to fulfil the real or anticipated needs of the population. Since the church was much too large to be maintained by a dwindling community, it was partly demolished in 1672, and some of the materials used to build a smaller thatched church within the remaining shell.

East Green,
Southwold

Although some of the nine 'greens', or open spaces, at Southwold were in existence long before the disastrous fire of 1659, which destroyed many of the houses, it is said that others were created as firebreaks during the rebuilding of the town. Among the places of interest near East Green are: the light-house, first lit in 1899 and more than 100 feet in height; the brewery, famous for Adnam's Ale, sometimes delivered locally by horse-drawn dray; and the Sole Bay Inn, named after the battle of Sole (Southwold) Bay, which was fought between the Anglo-French and Dutch fleets in 1672. The Bay, the anchorage of the English fleet, has since been removed by coastal erosion. The fifteenth-century church of St Edmund, one of the few medieval buildings to survive the fire, is, according to Pevsner, the 'epitome of Suffolk flushwork' (knapped flint and stone in deco-rative patterns on the exterior). 'Southwold Jack', like 'Jack-o'-the-Clock' in Blythburgh church, is a painted wooden bell-striking figure, now used to signal the start of the service.

Maritime Museum,
Lowestoft

The Lowestoft Maritime Museum – located at the entrance to Sparrow's Nest Park in the north part of the town – is housed in a small fisherman's flint-built cottage and contains exhibits relating to the town's seafaring history (notably the fishing industry, which saw its heyday during the late nine-teenth and early twentieth cen-turies). Also in the park, the Royal Naval Patrol Service Museum displays items connect-ed with the service, including photographs, documents, uni-forms and model ships. The High Light, overlooking both museums, was built in 1874. It stands on the site of the first lighthouse in England to be erected by Trinity House. Built by 1609, it was itself replaced by the lighthouse known as 'Pepys' Tower' (due to it having been built in 1676, the first year in which Samuel Pepys was Master of Trinity House). The Low Light – which stood on the beach and was not only designed to be moved, but was rebuilt on numerous occasions because of coastal erosion and the move-ment of sands offshore – was finally demolished in 1922.

Saxtead Green Mill

Standing beside the village green, some three miles west of Framlingham, the white weather-boarded Saxtead Green Mill is considered to be the finest surviving example of the most advanced type of post mill built anywhere in the world. Erected in the eighteenth century – on the site of an earlier corn mill – the windmill has two distinct parts: the upper 'buck' (or main body); and the lower brick round-house, which has been raised in height several times over subsequent years. Being the oldest type of windmill, post mills often appear in medieval iconography. One of the earliest is on a fourteenth-century boss in the vaulted roof of the cloisters of Norwich Cathedral Priory. The miller is depicted riding his horse with a sack on his back. This is a medieval 'stupid miller' joke based on the saying 'a merciful man is merciful to his beast.' For by carrying the sack, he believes that he is lightening his animal's load. The tools of the miller's trade may also be illustrated, as on the gravestone of the millwright, Thomas Smith (d. 1725), in Wiveton churchyard.

Thornham Parva Church

Deep in the midst of the Suffolk countryside – seven miles south of Diss – the tiny thatched church of St Mary at Thornham Parva contains some remarkable medieval treasures that have only been revealed in recent times. The fourteenth-century painted retable behind the altar was discovered in the loft of a nearby stable in 1927, and may have originally formed part of the high altar of a monastery at Thetford. The wall paintings, once obscured by darkened wax, are thought to date from the early fourteenth century and depict, on the south and north walls, respectively, the infancy of Christ and the death of St Edmund. Some of the scenes, like Edmund's martyrdom, have been wholly or partly destroyed by the subsequent insertion of windows into the walls. In the scene where the cart carrying the saint's relics is miraculously able to cross a bridge that is far too narrow for it, the rounded arch of the north doorway is imaginatively used to represent the bridge. More paintings, however, remain hidden behind the eighteenth-century gallery that fills the west end.

Parish Church & Guildhall,
Eye

Dedicated to St Peter and St Paul, the parish church at Eye, considered to be one of the finest in Suffolk, is particularly celebrated for its majestic late fifteenth-century tower – 110 feet high and panelled from top to bottom in flushwork. The timber-framed Guildhall, beside it, was built at around the same time, but was extensively restored in 1875. From *c.* 1495 until 1965 it housed the town grammar school. On top of the mound, opposite, are the ruins of the castle, built by William Malet between 1066 and 1071. The elliptical shape of the castle bailey, with the motte at the eastern end, is still apparent in the lay-out of the present town. In *c.* 1561, long after the castle had become redundant, a windmill was erected on the motte, where it remained until its demolition in 1844. The Benedictine priory, founded by Malet's son, Robert, stood outside the town, on the eastern banks of the River Dove. The site, with sparse remains, is now occupied by a farm. The name 'Eye' is derived from the Old English word for 'island'.

Wingfield Castle

Built by Michael de la Pole, Lord Chancellor of England (who received his licence to crenellate in 1384), Wingfield Castle was extensively rebuilt in *c.* 1545. The turrets of the central gatehouse, rising 60 feet above the moat, and the walls and corner towers either side, are survivals of the original building. The Chancellor's son, another Michael de la Pole and 2nd Earl of Suffolk (d. 1415), built the Lady Chapel in the church of St Andrew. His tomb is also in the church. The oldest stone monument is that of Sir John Wingfield, who helped his close friend, the Black Prince, defeat the French army at the battle of Poitiers in 1356. He vowed to found a college with money raised from French ransoms, but was struck down by the plague in 1361. His wife, however, founded the college in his name the following year. Although it was turned into an oddly proportioned Georgian country house in the late eighteenth century, the medieval Great Hall of the original manor is preserved inside. Today, Wingfield Old College is home to Wingfield Arts.

Leiston Abbey

Originally founded in 1182 on Minsmere Marshes by Ranulph de Glanville, Lord Chief Justice, the abbey for Premonstratensian canons near Leiston, was removed to its present site – on higher ground, a mile or so inland – in 1363 because of persistent incursions by the sea. After its partial destruction by fire in *c.* 1380, the monastery was rebuilt on a much grander scale. Among its extensive remains, now in the care of English Heritage, is the thatched Lady Chapel, restored as a house of prayer in the early twentieth century. Dominating the coastline, a few miles to the south-east, are the controversial silhouettes of the Sizewell A and B power stations, where visitors are introduced to the wonders of nuclear energy and Geiger counters click impatiently. The coast near Leiston, particularly the former gap through the cliffs at Sizewell, was extremely popular with smugglers, especially the notorious Hadleigh Gang, who operated – during the peak of their activities in the eighteenth century – from the market town of that name, 30 miles inland.

Woodbridge Tide Mill

Dominating the riverside frontage of the old market town and port at Woodbridge, the white weather-boarded tide mill on the Deben dates from 1793, although there have been mills on the site since at least 1170. During the Middle Ages, it belonged to the Augustinian canons of Woodbridge priory, founded by Ernald Rufus in the closing years of the twelfth century. The present mill, used to grind flour as well as meal for animal feed, ceased working in 1957 when the waterwheel's 22-inch-thick oak axle-shaft broke. When Jean Gardner purchased the mill and adjacent granary in 1968, the buildings were in imminent danger of collapse. It is entirely due to the efforts of the Woodbridge Tide Mill Trust and its 'Friends', that the mill and machinery have now been fully restored. Since most of the original mill pond had been converted into a yacht marina, a new one was constructed. Known as 'Wyllie's Pool' (after the Friends Hon. Secretary, Peter Wyllie), it can store enough water at high tide to power the mill for about half an hour at low tide.

Flatford Mill

Born at East Bergholt on 11 June 1776, John Constable was the fourth child of Golding Constable, a prosperous miller, and his wife Anne. Although he was expected to take over his father's business, Constable wanted to be a painter. In 1821, long after achieving his ambition, he admitted in a letter to his friend John Fisher, that it was the scenes of his 'careless boyhood' along 'the banks of the Stour' that made him want to paint landscapes. 'I had often thought of pictures of them,' he added, 'before I had ever touched a pencil.' One of the many subjects he painted in the area of East Bergholt and the lower Stour valley (known as 'Constable Country' even in his lifetime), was Flatford Mill, one of two mills owned by his father (the other being Dedham). Built in c. 1733, the water-powered mill was used to grind corn into flour. The adjoining timber-framed miller's house (now covered by a brick façade) was the original Constable family home. Today the mill is owned by the National Trust, but since 1944 it has been leased to the Field Studies Council.

Guildhall & Church,
Hadleigh

Situated on the River Brett, a tributary of the Stour, the ancient market town of Hadleigh derives its name from the Old English for 'the heather-covered forest clearing'. During the ninth century, the Anglo-Saxon settlement became a Danish stronghold. Indeed Guthrum (baptized Athelstan), King of the Danish kingdom of East Anglia, was buried in the town in 890. During the fourteenth and fifteenth centuries, because of its woollen cloth industry, Hadleigh became one of the wealthiest towns in East Anglia. The flint and freestone St Mary's, rebuilt towards the end of the fifteenth century, retains the tower of the earlier and smaller parish church. It is crowned by an elegant timber-framed, lead-covered spire. The Guildhall, another monument to the cloth trade, dates from the 1430s, when the central, three-storey section was built as the Market House. The brick-built Deanery Tower, immediately west of the church, was built as the gatehouse to Archdeacon Pykenham's planned grand residence (which was never built) in 1495.

Willy Lott's Cottage,
Flatford

Built in *c.* 1600, Willy Lott's Cottage, facing Flatford Mill, has been made world-famous by one of Constable's most reproduced and celebrated paintings, The Haywain, now in the National Gallery. Painted in oils in 1821, it was this large canvas that brought Constable formal, but very belated recognition. Not in England (that did not happen until his election to the Royal Academy in 1829), but in France, where in 1824 the painting won a gold medal at the Paris Salon. The French critic, Charles Nodier – who had seen the painting earlier in London – considered that it was a painting 'with which the ancient or modern masters have very few masterpieces that could be put in opposition'. Willy Lott's Cottage (formerly Gibbeon's Gate Farm) appears in many of Constable's paintings, though he altered its shape to suit his composition. According to CR Leslie, Constable's friend and biographer, it was the birthplace of Willy Lott, who 'had passed more than eighty years without having spent four whole days from it'.

Hut Hill,
Knettishall Heath

Much of the Knettishall Heath Country Park's 375 acres of heathland, grassland and mixed woodland was designated as a Site of Special Scientific Interest in 1984 because of its ecological importance as a remnant of East Anglia's once-extensive Breckland landscape. Lying on the southern side of the Little Ouse River, nine miles upstream of Thetford, the acidic soils of the heath are dominated by wavy hair grass, heather and bracken. The presence of chalk in some areas, however, gives rise to quite different plant communities. Dating from the early Bronze Age (some 4,000 years ago), the Hut Hill burial mound was built after much of the former forest had been cleared. Three long-distance trails start at the park – the Peddars Way (to Holme-Next-the Sea), the Angles Way (to Great Yarmouth) and the Icknield Way (to the Chiltern Hills). They, in turn, are linked to the Norfolk Coast Path (from Holme to Cromer), the Weavers Way (from Cromer to Great Yarmouth) and the Ridgeway (from Ivinghoe Beacon, in the Chilterns, to Overton Hill, Wiltshire).

Kersey

Attractively lined with half-timbered and colour-washed cottages, the main street at Kersey plunges downhill on both sides to meet in a watersplash where, in spring, house martins gather wet mud from between the cobbles from which to make their nests. High on the hill above the village, the 'wool' church of St Mary's dates from the twelfth century, but was rebuilt and enlarged in the fourteenth and fifteenth centuries. Work, however, was interrupted because of the Black Death, which swept through the village in 1349 killing many of the inhabitants. Its battlemented flint tower was completed in 1481. Dating from Anglo-Saxon times, the village was granted the right to hold a weekly market in 1252 and, until the seventeenth century when the main centre of the woollen industry shifted to Yorkshire, it shared in the general prosperity of Suffolk's cloth trade. Tradition maintains that the village specialized in the type of cloth known as Kersey, but this is not supported by historical evidence. On the opposite side of the valley to the church are the remains of an Augustinian priory.

Guildhall & Church,
Stoke-by-Nayland

Immortalized in several paintings by Constable, the church of St Mary the Virgin at Stoke-by-Nayland stands high on a ridge overlooking the valley of the Stour. Rebuilt in Perpendicular style during the fifteenth century, with wealth from the local wool trade, the church is 168 feet long, with a massive west tower that rises 120 feet into the sky. Among the memorials to the Howard family, former owners of the Tendring estate and the village, is a brass to Catherine (d. 1465), wife of Sir John Howard, Duke of Norfolk, and the great-grandmother of two of Henry VIII's wives: Anne Boleyn and Catherine Howard. Although Tendring Hall has been demolished, the estate, covering almost 3,000 acres in and around the village, was covenanted to the National Trust in 1968 by Sir Joshua Rowley. In School Street, immediately to the west of the church, are two splendid half-timbered houses, both dating from the sixteenth century: the Guildhall and the Maltings. Nearby, Polstead was the scene of the famous Victorian crime – 'The Murder in the Red Barn' – solved by a dream.

St Mary's Church,
Cavendish

Nestling in the shadow of St Mary's church tower at Cavendish is a group of pink-washed thatched almshouses, known as 'Hyde Park Corner Cottages'. Although much restored, they date from the fourteenth century. The village – which stands on the north bank of the upper Ouse, three miles downstream of Clare – was once the main home of the Cavendish family (now the Dukes of Devonshire). Sir John Cavendish, Chief Justice of the King's Bench, left money in his will to rebuild the chancel of the church. Unfortunately, he was beheaded at Bury St Edmunds in 1381 because of his son's involvement in the killing of Wat Tyler – leader of the 'Peasants' Revolt'. Seeking revenge, Tyler's supporters descended on Cavendish, forcing the justice to flee. Apparently, before they caught up with him at Bury, the rebels found Sir John's valuables hidden in the church belfry. The tower of St Mary's dates from the early fourteenth century and supports a chimney as well as a stair turret.

Westleton Heath

Containing heathland, woodland, marshland, mudflats, saltlings and grazing meadows, the National Nature Reserve at Westleton Heath attracts such diverse species of birds as stone curlew, red-backed shrike, nightjar and woodlark. Its sandy soiled stretches of heather and bracken, known as the Sandlings, were grazed by sheep during medieval times and, for many years, were designated common land. As La Rochefoucauld observed in 1784: 'These lands are for the most part enormously extensive and are no use for anything but the sheep of those parishioners who have the right to send them there: worse, they are sometimes so much overgrown with bracken that they are good for absolutely nothing.' Another fine remnant of the Sandlings can be found, nearby, at Dunwich Heath, owned by the National Trust. The latter is adjoined to the south by the Minsmere (probably the most famous of all the R.S.P.B.'s reserves), containing a variety of wildlife habitats, including the shallow marshland lagoons of the Snape, reed beds, heathland and woodland.

Dunwich

One of the most dramatic examples of the destructive power of the sea is the loss of medieval Dunwich, once a major port with a harbour at the mouth of the Dunwich River, and now part of the tide-washed sand and shingle that constitutes the beach. Although the church of All Saints finally toppled into the sea in 1919, two gravestones from its cemetery still stand precariously on the cliff edge. Most of the houses in the present village date from the eighteenth century. The church of St James is nineteenth century. While the ruins of the leper hospital and the Franciscan priory are medieval. The seat of East Anglia's first bishopric was established at Dunwich by St Felix in c. 630. In the thirteenth century the town was the largest port in Suffolk, with some 80 trading vessels, eight or nine parish churches and several religious houses. Although the sea had already begun to take its toll, the port's final demise was brought about by the great storm of 1328, which irrevocably blocked the haven entrance with millions of tons of sand and shingle.

Outer Harbour,
Lowestoft

Lowestoft, Britain's easternmost port, is divided into two parts by Lake Lothing – the narrow stretch of water that connects the North Sea to Oulton Broad and the Broadland waterway network. The bridge, which links both parts of the town, can be raised to allow large sea-going vessels to move between the inner and outer harbours. Although the town's origins date back at least to Anglo-Saxon times, it did not become a prosperous fishing and commercial port until around the middle of the nineteenth century, when the harbour was constructed and an inland navigation route opened to Norwich. The arrival of the railway in 1847 – which took freshly caught fish (mainly herrings) to markets, first at Norwich, and eventually London, Manchester and the Midlands – led to the town's rapid expansion. On the north side of the town are the 'Scores', steep paths that ran between the original cliff-top and shore settlements (the latter is now an industrial zone). The main holiday resort area and beaches are south of the bridge and harbour.

COLCHESTER AND ESSEX

Hadleigh Castle

Strategically situated on a high ridge overlooking the Thames estuary and Essex marshes, the castle at Hadleigh was built by Hubert de Burgh, Justiciar of England, shortly after receiving Henry III's approval in 1230. After the death in 1219 of William Marshall (regent for the king in his minority from 1216), de Burgh became the most powerful man in the kingdom. His dramatic fall in 1232 was effectively brought about by his bitterest enemy Peter des Roches, Bishop of Winchester, who won the king's favour after returning to England from a crusade. De Burgh was stripped of all his offices and Welsh possessions and imprisoned on charges of treason. Although he was eventually pardoned and reconciled with the king, de Burgh never regained his power and died in forced retirement in 1243. Hadleigh castle was essentially rebuilt by Edward III in the 1360s. Originally the high curtain wall contained eight towers and a defensive gatehouse, or barbican. Today, much of the fortress has been lost by landslips on the southern side.

Laying claim to being Britain's oldest recorded town, Colchester (known as *Camulodunum*, 'the fortress of the Celtic war god, Camulos') was the tribal capital of the Trinovantes when the troops of Julius Caesar first invaded the island in 55 BC. On their return the following year in much greater numbers, the Romans stormed through south-east England, crossed the River Thames and, with the help of the Trinovantes, captured the main stronghold of the Catuvellauni (possibly Wheathampstead in Hertfordshire). In about AD 7 the leader of the Catuvellauni, Cunobelinus (Shakespeare's Cymbeline), conquered the Trinovantes and made *Camulodunum* the capital of his greatly expanded kingdom. Developing into one of the largest and richest centres in Iron Age Britain, the sprawling settlement (or *oppidum*) covered an area of some 12 square miles, and was protected to the north and east by the River Colne, to the south by the Roman River and to the west by a series of defensive earthworks, including the surviving three-mile-long Gryme's Dyke. In addition to maintaining friendly relations with Rome, Cunobelinus actively encouraged trade between his kingdom and the Roman empire. Indeed, it is thought that he established a virtual monopoly on the traffic in goods from the continent. His wealth and power, which extended over most of south-east England, was such that one classical author called him the 'King of the Britons'. After his death in AD 41, Cunobelinus was succeeded by his sons Caratacus and Togodumnus, who apparently did not share his pro-Roman views. But it was Cunobelinus's exile of another of his sons, Adminius, the previous year that drew Rome's attention to the growing tribal unrest in Britain and persuaded the unpredictable Emperor Gaius (Caligula) to accept that the time was ripe for invasion.

Assembling his troops on the Channel shore of the European mainland, Gaius is reputed to have cancelled the invasion and commanded his men to collect sea shells instead. In AD 41, shortly after declaring himself a god, Gaius was murdered by soldiers of the Praetorian Guard. Given Gaius's instability and the damage he caused to Roman prestige, his successor, Claudius, needed to prove that he was fit to rule as emperor. To stay alive he had to win the respect and, therefore, the allegiance of the army. A successful invasion of Britain seemed the obvious solution. Landing unopposed at Richborough, north-east Kent, in AD 43, the invading Romans, under Aulus Plautius, pushed inland, overcoming all resistance from the British tribes and, at a crossing of the River Medway, decisively defeated the forces of Caratacus and Togodumnus. Togodumnus was subsequently killed, while Caratacus fled west to emerge later as the leader of the warlike Silures of south Wales, stubbornly resisting the might of the Roman army until his eventual defeat and capture in AD 51.

After crossing the Medway, Aulus Plautius halted the advance to consolidate his position and to bring up reinforcements, including elephants. Their arrival conveniently coincided with the arrival of the Emperor Claudius, who took over command and not only led the army across the Thames and into the heart of Cunobelinus's former kingdom, but rode in triumph into the legendary capital of *Camulodunum* itself, where he ceremoniously accepted the surrender of the south-eastern tribes, including the Catuvellauni and the Trinovantes. To commemorate their conquest, the Romans built a colossal temple, dedicated to Claudius, which became the focus of local resentment and hatred. In AD 60 Boudicca (Boadicea) – the newly widowed queen of Prasutagus, King of the Iceni – was flogged and her daughters raped by Roman officials. Outraged, the Iceni of East Anglia, led by their queen, rose in rebellion against Roman tyranny and oppression. Joined by the Trinovantes, they marched on the newly built, but defenceless, *colonia* (a colony for retired Roman soldiers) at *Camulodunum* and razed it to the ground, massacring all who stood in their way, including those who had taken refuge in the temple. Boudicca succeeded in destroying *Londinium* (London) and *Verulamium* (St Albans) before her rebellion was crushed at a battle in the Midlands. Although, Boudicca managed to escape, she died soon afterward: either by suicide or from sickness. Roman vengeance under Gaius Suetonius Paulinus was terrible. Everyone suspected of supporting the uprising, even those who had remained neutral, were slaughtered and their tribal lands laid to waste. It was only after Paulinus (who had vowed to hunt down every last rebel) had been recalled to Rome that peace gradually returned to East Anglia. *Camulodunum* was rebuilt as a fortified town encircled by walls 16 feet high and some nine feet thick. Much of the wall's circuit of nearly two miles is still visible. But the most impressive relic of the Roman town to survive is the Balkerne Gate, the main entrance to the *colonia* from London.

During the Anglo-Saxon period, the town changed its name to Colchester, meaning 'the former Roman town on the River Colne'. Although never regaining its pre-Roman glory, it was an important medieval market town, cloth-making centre and port, boasting an immense castle keep and two major monasteries. The Civil War siege of 1648 reduced much of the town to rubble. Today, re-used Roman bricks and stones can be traced in many of the buildings, serving as a haunting reminder that Colchester's long and eventful past still lingers in the present.

Dovercourt Lighthouse, *Harwich*

The two unusual screw-pile lighthouses on the foreshore at Dovercourt were built to replace the Harwich High and Low Lights in 1863. Connected by a concrete causeway, the lighthouses were of a revolutionary new design, first brought into service by Trinity House on the Maplin Sands, near Southend, in 1858. Their strength lay in the fact that, compared with the more conventional solid structures, the iron legs (firmly planted in hard rock) offered less resistance to wind and waves and were, as a result, less likely to be damaged. It was a design that was particularly suited to locations that were regularly washed by the tide, such as sandbanks and foreshores. When brought into line, the Dovercourt lights (like the High and Low Lights) marked the shipping passage into Harwich harbour by guiding the vessels clear of the shifting sandbanks offshore. When the Harwich High and Low Lights ceased to align with the shoals they were renamed 'misleading lights'. The Dovercourt lights became redundant in 1917, when the passage into the harbour was marked with lighted buoys.

Mistley Towers

The two neo-classical towers of the church of St Mary at Mistley, on the banks of the Stour estuary, are a rare example of the ecclesiastical architecture of Robert Adam. Although the church was completed only in 1735, the MP and Paymaster General of the Armed Forces, Robert Rigby of Mistley Hall, commissioned Adam to remodel it, resulting in the addition of the towers in 1776. Originally standing at the east and west ends of the church, they were saved (apparently to be turned into mausoleums) when the nave between them was demolished in 1870. Adam also designed the two lodges, built in 1782 that stood at the entrance to Mistley Hall. It was from the river port and boat-building centre of Mistley that Golding Constable shipped flour from his mills at Dedham and Flatford to London. In some of his son's paintings and drawings of Dedham Vale and the Stour estuary, the twin towers of Mistley's church can be clearly identified.

The Crown House,
Newport

During the sixteenth and seventeenth centuries, pargeting – external decorative plasterwork applied to timber-framed buildings (in relief and inscribed) – was especially popular in Essex and Suffolk. The Crown House in Bridge End at Newport, a small village on the River Cam about three miles south-west of Saffron Walden, is one of many fine examples of the plasterers' craft. Although dated 1692, the house is of late sixteenth- or early seventeenth-century origin. Above the front door, and beneath the crown from which the house takes its name, is a large shell-hood. Monk's Barn, in the main street, is a fifteenth-century house with exposed timber-framing infilled by brick nogging. It has a carving of the Virgin and two ministering angels beneath the oriel window. The large flint church of St Mary the Virgin, formerly collegiate, dates from the thirteenth century. Among the items of interest inside is a rare altar chest of the same date containing paintings of the crucifixion, the Virgin and several saints. It now serves as a communion table.

St Andrew's Church,
Greensted

Standing on the site of a seventh-century foundation, and possibly an even earlier pagan place of worship, the timbers of the church of St Andrew's at Greensted, near Chipping Ongar, have been scientifically dated to reveal that the Anglo-Saxon building was constructed in *c*. 850 – making it the oldest wooden church in the world. Like most parish churches, however, it has been considerably altered and extended over the centuries. The only part of the Anglo-Saxon church to survive are the walls of the nave, built of oak logs split in halves and positioned vertically in an oak sill. In 1848, because of decay, the timbers were shortened and footed on a sill of brick to maintain their original height. The rest of the church was extensively restored at the same time. In *c*. 1500, when the south porch was added and the chancel rebuilt in brick, the thatched roof of the nave was tiled and given three dormer windows. The timber tower, weather-boarded in typical Essex style, dates from the seventeenth century, and possibly earlier.

Almshouses and Windmill,
Thaxted

Standing near the parish church at Thaxted are two rows of almshouses and a brick-built windmill. The thatched single-storey almshouse, known as the Chantry, was originally built as a priest's house. In 1933 it was in a derelict condition, but has since been restored and converted into a single residence. The tiled row, with its bargeboarded north gable, was built as an almshouse in *c*. 1714, with eight 'one up and one down' dwellings to accommodate sixteen poor old people. In 1975 it was renovated and converted into three separate dwellings for elderly couples. The tower windmill was erected in 1804 by John Webb, a local farmer and the owner of the brick works from which much of the construction material came. It now contains a small museum. Thaxted's medieval prosperity is reflected in the cathedral-like church of St John the Baptist, St Mary and St Laurence, built on its hill-top site between 1340 and 1510. The impressive timber-framed guildhall, in the town centre, is jettied on three sides and was built by the Guild of Cutlers in *c*. 1390.

The Turf Maze,
Saffron Walden

The largest surviving ancient labyrinth in England is cut into the turf of the Common (formerly Castle Green) at Saffron Walden. First recorded in 1699, its unique design consists of a series of 17 concentric circles, divided by turnings into a cross, with four projecting round corners known as 'bastions', 'bellows' or 'ears'. Constructed within an earth bank and ditch, the diameter of the largest circle is approximately 90 feet, while across the bastions it measures 132 feet. The pathway, which was lined with some 6,400 bricks in 1911, is reputed to be a mile in length. At the centre there was once an ash tree, but this was destroyed on Guy Fawkes night in 1823. In the eighteenth and nineteenth centuries young men used to compete in a sporting event that involved racing round the pathway to reach a girl in the centre. Tradition holds that the maze is a copy of a much larger labyrinth that once existed close by. The Victorian yew hedge maze at Bridge End Gardens was officially reopened in 1991, having been replanted.

Church Walk,
Saffron Walden

During the Middle Ages, the wool and market town of Walden (also known as Chipping Walden to distinguish it from other places with the same name) was a centre for the cultivation of saffron (*crocus sativus*), used primarily as a natural yellow dye. Towards the end of the fifteenth century, in recognition of the value of the plant's commercial importance, the town began to be called Saffron Walden – a name confirmed the following century by the inclusion of the flowering crocus in its coat of arms. The saffron is also depicted in the magnificent church of St Mary the Virgin, rebuilt on the profits of the wool and cloth trade in the fifteenth and sixteenth centuries. Almost 200 feet in length, it is one of the largest parish churches in Essex. The total height of the tower and spire is 193 feet. The Old Sun Inn, in Church Street, is noted for its impressive seventeenth-century pargeting, which depicts the legendary Tom Hickathrift fighting the Wisbech giant: the latter carrying a club, and the former using the wheel of a cart for a shield and its axle as a weapon.

The Round Church,
Little Maplestead

The parish church of St John the Baptist at Little Maplestead, three miles north of the market town of Halstead, is one of only five surviving medieval round churches in England (the others are at Cambridge, Northampton, Ludlow Castle and the Temple in London). It is also the smallest. Built in *c.* 1335 by the Knights of St John of Jerusalem, or the Knights Hospitallers, its design was based on the church of the Holy Sepulchre at Jerusalem. Drastically restored in 1851-7, the church consists of a fourteenth-century chancel, with a semi-circular apse, and a 30-feet-diameter nave and aisle, surmounted by a six-sided belfry. The porch and vestry are Victorian additions. Although the present structure stands on possibly the site of the first church (built primarily for the Knights own use after the foundation of the Preceptory in the late twelfth century), the location of Little Maplestead's former parish church, built in early Norman times, is unknown. The font, with its rough carvings and deep bowl, is thought to have come from this church.

Finchingfield

Finchingfield contains all the elements of the quintessential English scene: a winding street leading to a small bridge and a central green; houses on different levels and in different styles climbing gently from the village pond to the Norman tower of the parish church; several public houses, including the Finch Inn; and an eighteenth-century weather-boarded post mill. The bell-cote, on top of the square tower of the mainly fourteenth-century church of St John the Baptist, dates from the eighteenth century. The angelus bell inside is all that survives of the lofty leaded spire that once crowned the tower. Access to the church-yard from the street can be gained through the arch of the fifteenth-century guildhall. The thatched six-sided Round House, on the village outskirts, was built by the owner of nearby Spains Hall in the late eighteenth century. A memorial in the church to William Kempe (d. 1628) – whose ancestors built the Elizabethan Hall – records his self-imposed seven-year penance of silence for wrongly accusing his wife of infidelity.

Prior's Hall Barn,
Widdington

Built in the late-fourteenth century to store grain and other agricultural produce, Prior's Hall Barn at Widdington, two miles south-east of Newport, is one of the finest surviving timber-framed barns in England. Eight bays long, with low external walls, side aisles, horizontal tie-beams, vertical king-posts and a crown-post roof, it is an outstanding example of the medieval carpenters' craft. By bearing much of the weight of the roof on aisle posts, positioned on either side of a long central nave, the width of the barn could be significantly increased. Since this type of construction was imported from Europe, aisled barns are mainly found nearest the Continent in eastern and southern England. The largest and most impressive example is the stone-built Great Coxwell tithe barn in Oxfordshire, now owned by the National Trust. William Morris, who lived at nearby Kelmscott Manor, thought it was 'the finest piece of architecture in England, as beautiful as a cathedral'. Prior's Hall Barn, extensively restored, is now in the care of English Heritage.

Borley Church

Close to the Suffolk border, the straggling village of Borley has the dubious reputation of being the most haunted place in Britain. Although inexplicable phenomena have been reported in the vicinity of the church and churchyard, they were originally centred around the rectory, built on the site of a former monastery by the Rev. Henry Bull in 1863. Even after its destruction by fire in 1939, the 'hauntings' persisted. Local legend maintains that a monk from the monastery fell in love with a nun from a nearby convent. As a punishment for attempting to elope together, the monk was hanged and the nun bricked up alive in the monastic cellars. The Bull family, who lived in the rectory until 1927, reported many sightings of a ghostly nun, particularly in the rectory grounds and along a path known as the 'Nun's Walk'. Despite doubts cast on the integrity of Harry Price, the psychical researcher who carried out a prolonged investigation into strange occurrences at the rectory, Borley seems to be stuck with its 'haunted' reputation.

Audley End

In 1697 Celia Fiennes visited Audley End, one mile west of Saffron Walden, and noted in her 'Journeys' that the mansion, with '750 rooms', 'makes a noble appearance like a town, so many towers and buildings of stone within a park which is walled round'. Standing on the site of Walden Abbey, granted to Sir Thomas Audley after its dissolution in 1538, the house was built on a palatial scale between 1605 and 1614 by Thomas Howard, Earl of Suffolk, who became Lord High Treasurer of England in 1614. Apparently, James I remarked that the house was 'too large for a king, but might do for a Lord Treasurer'. After being sold to Charles II in 1667, Audley End was used occasionally by successive monarchs until 1701, when it returned to the Howard family. The present house, owned by English Heritage, is the result of much demolition, partial rebuilding and substantial redecoration in the latter half of the eighteenth century. 'Capability' Brown laid out the grounds, while Robert Adam – whose work can also be seen in the house – designed several of the garden monuments.

Church Path, Wendens Ambo

In 1662 the two neighbouring parishes of Great Wenden (Wenden Magna) and Little Wenden (Wenden Parva) were amalgamated to form Wendens Ambo, meaning 'both Wendens'. As the new parish was too small to support two ecclesiastical centres, St Mary the Virgin at Great Wenden became the sole place of worship and the church at Little Wenden was abandoned and, eventually, demolished. Dating from the early Norman period, the church at Great Wenden was altered and enlarged in the thirteenth, fourteenth and fifteenth centuries. The rebuilding of the north aisle and the extension to the south aisle were carried out during Victorian times. On top of the Norman tower is a slender spire, or spike, more commonly found across the border in Hertfordshire. The arch of the west doorway is made of Roman bricks, thought to have come from the remains of a villa that stood about half-a-mile away. Lining Church Path, the road leading to the church, are a row of attractive colour-washed cottages, some thatched, others tiled.

Layer Marney Tower

Acclaimed as the 'tallest Tudor gatehouse in the country', Layer Marney Tower – seven miles south-west of Colchester – was begun by Henry, 1st Lord Marney, in the early years of Henry VIII's reign. Although designed as part of a magnificent new residence, Lord Marney's death in 1523 (followed by the death of his son, John, two years later) saw only the completion of the gatehouse, its east and west wings and an isolated south range – almost all of the buildings that survive today. Although the envisaged courtyard and accompanying buildings were never built, Henry and his son made provision in their wills for the nearby parish church of St Mary the Virgin (started at the same time as the house) to be finished. Architecturally, the tower is celebrated for its innovative use of brick and the newly fashionable Italian material, terracotta (stone was a rare and expensive commodity in Essex, the soil of which is essentially clay). Other attractions at Layer Marney include a collection of rare-breed farm animals, a deer park and formal gardens.

Colchester Castle

Using some imported stone, but mainly recycled building materials from the extensive ruins of the Roman *colonia* (colony) at *Camulodunum* (the tribal centre of the Iron Age Trinovantes), the conquering Normans constructed a massive castle at Colchester to protect their newly won territories. All that now remains of the fortress, begun in *c.* 1076, is the massive rectangular keep – the largest in the whole of Europe – measuring 151 feet by 110 feet, with walls originally some 90 feet high and more than 12 feet thick. In fact, the three- or four-storey structure (of which only two now survive) was built on the foundations of a huge Roman temple dedicated to the Emperor Claudius. The walls of the Norman keep were originally faced with stone, but much of the rubble core is now exposed. In addition to Roman bricks and dressed stone, the walls also contain locally quarried 'septaria' (smooth clay-limestone nodules of the London clay). Roofed over in 1934-5, the castle keep is now a museum, housing exhibits and displays of Colchester's history.

St Botolph's Priory,
Colchester

One of several religious houses in Colchester, including the Benedictine abbey of St John, St Botolph's Priory was originally an Anglo-Saxon foundation, served by a small community of secular priests. In 1093 it became the first house in England to adopt the Augustinian rule and, as such, was granted many privileges. Nevertheless, despite having authority over all other English houses of the Order, it was never wealthy. After its dissolution in 1536, most of the monastic buildings were demolished for their building material. The nave of the priory church was saved, however, and served as the town's principal church until it was itself destroyed during the Civil War siege of Colchester in 1648. Like the castle, it has lost its surface covering, revealing the recycled Roman brick used in its construction. The present church of St Botolph, standing beside the ruins of the old, was built in the Norman style in 1837. All that remains of St John's Abbey, founded in 1096 and dissolved in 1539, is the fifteenth-century gatehouse, which also bears scars from the Civil War.

St Peter-on-the-Wall,
Bradwell

Standing in lonely isolation on the site of the Roman shore fort of *Orthona*, some two miles north-east of the church of St Thomas at Bradwell-on-Sea, the chapel of St Peter-on-the-Wall was part of a Celtic monastery founded in AD 654 by St Cedd, the Bishop of the East Saxons (who also founded the monasteries of Tilbury, Essex and Lastingham, North Yorkshire). The first church, probably timber-built, was soon replaced by the present chapel, constructed with stone from the ruined fort. Since it was dedicated to St Peter and stood astride the western wall of the Roman fort, it came to be known as St Peter-on-the Wall. In 664, at the Synod of Whitby, Cedd abandoned the Celtic for the Roman observances. Later that same year, he died of the plague and was buried at Lastingham. During the thirteenth century, St Peter's became a chapel-of-ease to St Thomas's at Bradwell. Sadly, it was partly demolished in the seventeenth century and turned into a barn. The nave, all that now remains, was restored and reconsecrated in 1920.

St Osyth's Priory

Located amidst winding creeks and marshland, three miles west of Clacton-on-Sea, the first monastery at the village of St Osyth (formerly called Chich) was founded as a nunnery in the seventh century by St Osyth, the wife of Sighere, King of the East Saxons. Legend says that the saint and first abbess was slain by marauding Danes in 653. Apparently, her body was taken to Aylesbury, but by the beginning of the eleventh century it had been re-enshrined at Chich. Dedicated to St Peter, St Paul and St Osyth, the monastery was refounded in 1121 as a priory for Augustinian canons by Richard de Belmeis, Bishop of London. After its elevation to the status of an abbey in *c.* 1161, the foundation rapidly flourished, gaining an international reputation for piety and learning. It was dissolved in 1539. Today, the remains have been incorporated into a private house (known as St Osyth's Priory). The most impressive survival is the flint, brick and stone gatehouse of *c.* 1475. Set within extensive grounds, the Priory houses an impressive art collection in the Georgian wing.

Hornbeams,
Hatfield Forest

Once part of the Royal Forest of Essex – a hunting preserve for medieval monarchs that extended over nearly all of the county – Hatfield Forest, comprising more than 1,000 acres of ancient woodland, is now in the care of the National Trust and has been designated a Site of Special Scientific Interest. In *Trees and Woodland in the British Landscape* (1976) Oliver Rackham claimed that in England it was 'the only place where one can step back into the Middle Ages to see, with a small effort of imagination, what a Forest looked like in use'. In addition to scrub, coppiced woodland, trees grown for timber and pollarded hawthorns, hornbeams and oaks, the 'forest' contains grazing plains, fen, stretches of open water, and wide grassy rides, or chases. The Houblons, a Huguenot family, created the lake in the mid eighteenth century by damming the Shermore Brook. They also built the Shell House on its banks and, over the next hundred years, planted many ornamental trees. Today the forest, which contains several prehistoric and Roman sites, is still inhabited by deer, mainly fallow.

Southend Pier

Stretching across the flats of the Thames estuary for 7,080 feet, or one mile and 600 yards, the seaside pier at Southend is the longest in the world. Built of iron in 1889, it replaced an earlier pier that was once described as 'a wooden sea-serpent centipede'. The only part of the old pier to be incorporated into the new structure was the Victorian brick entrance, which was demolished during the modernization programme of 1931. To cater for the ever-increasing number of passenger steamers wishing to call at Southend, the pier was extended in 1897. The last pier extension was completed in 1929. Over the years, the pier has suffered from a series of calamities, the latest being the explosion that destroyed the bowling alley on 7 June 1995. Ironically, the alley was erected on the ashes of the Pier Pavilion, burnt down in 1959. At least nine ships have collided with the pier, including the *Kingsabbey*, which sliced through the structure in 1986, causing a 70-feet gap. The most severe disaster, however, was the Pier Head fire of 1976.

Lightship,
Tollesbury

Overlooking the sheltered creeks, tidal marshes and open estuary of the River Blackwater, the former Trinity House lightvessel – moored in Woodrolfe Creek at Tollesbury and appropriately named *Trinity* – now belongs to Fellowship Afloat. This charitable trust provides residential outdoor activity courses as well as owning 150 acres of the surrounding saltings. The ship, which boasts a helipad, has been fitted out as an adventure-holiday base, complete with saloon, galley, 36 beds and all modern conveniences. As a safe harbour, once used for ship-building, Tollesbury marina is popular with boating and sailing enthusiasts. Although the town's main industry was the dredging of oysters, the arrival of the railway in 1907 encouraged wealthy Londoners to moor their large yachts in the harbour. As a consequence, the fishermen found themselves much in demand as crewmen (albeit seasonal). The tall, timber sail-lofts, dating from this period, still stand on the waterfront. One of the lofts is now used as an office by Fellowship Afloat.

PHOTOGRAPHIC NOTES

Salthouse Church

Dedicated to St Nicholas, the patron saint of fishermen, the parish church at Salthouse was rebuilt by Sir Henry Heydon between 1497 and 1503, incorporating the thirteenth-century tower of the previous structure. Sir Henry, incidentally, was the son of Sir John Heydon, who built the fortified manor house, Baconsthorpe Castle, near Holt. Charles Linnell, in his Salthouse church guide, suggests that the windows in the north and south aisles may be unusually narrow because of the very exposed location of the building, high on a ridge above the sea. It seems that gale force winds might well have damaged the windows had they been larger. In fact, until its restoration in 1932, the great east window was partially blocked up for many years. The graffiti on the back of the choir stalls is thought to have been carried out by children when the church was used as a school. Although crude, the drawings of ships are a reminder that Salthouse was once a busy port, until the 'Mayne Channel' leading to the sea was effectively blocked by an artificial bank in 1637.

My first introduction to the photographic potential of East Anglia and the Fens was brought about by having to include the region in *English Landscapes*, a prestigious book celebrating the ten-year partnership of Talbot and Whiteman. Limited by time, space and weather, I was able to explore only a small part of the region. Just enough to show the diversity that England offers, east to west and north to south. But my appetite was whetted. When the time came for me to start work on *East Anglia and the Fens* for the 'Country Series', I knew the book was to be something special.

Different regions of England each have their own distinguishing characteristics. East Anglia and the Fens is no exception. Flat and uninteresting it certainly is not! The weather, which is so often shaped by the lie of the land, nearly always produced a light of rare and beautiful quality. Dull and grey it certainly was not!

The photographs of East Anglia and the Fens take on an extra special significance when it is understood that much of the landscape is under threat of encroachment by the sea. Delicate fenlands, vibrant lavender fields, peaceful saltmarshes and tidal creeks acquire a new dimension. So many pretty villages and ancient churches become that more precious because of their seeming vulnerability. As do miles and miles of valuable farmlands and waterways. Preventative steps are being taken, such as the construction of defensive barriers of rock offshore at Eccles and Sea Palling, but will such measures be enough? Will image-makers of tomorrow even be able to see the scenes we take for granted today?

The photographic equipment used for this book was a Hasselblad medium format camera with 50mm, 80mm and 150mm lenses and a Nikon 35mm camera with 28mm(PC), 35mm, 85mm and 180mm lenses. A Linhof tripod was used with both systems. The filters were of the slight-warming 81 series. Polarizing filters and graduated neutral density filters were used to help the film record accurately the scenes as I saw them. The film was Fuji Provia for the Hasselblad and Fuji Velvia for the Nikon.

George, my border collie, continues to be my constant travelling companion. My experiences in the dry as well as watery landscape of East Anglia and the Fens may have been especially memorable, but to George it was a period of high adventure, one that surpassed even his wildest dreams! But that's a different story.

Rob Talbot

SELECTED PROPERTIES AND REGIONAL OFFICES

ENGLISH HERITAGE
All English Heritage properties, except where specified, are open from April to the end of October every day from 10am to 6pm (summer season); from November to end of March opening times are Wednesdays to Sundays from 10am to 4pm. The properties are closed on 24-26 December and 1 January.

Head Office
Keysign House
429 Oxford Street
London W1R 2HD
Tel: (0171) 973 3000

Midlands Regional Office
Hazelrigg House
33 Marefair
Northampton NN1 1SR
Tel: (01604) 730320

Audley End House & Park
Saffron Walden
Essex CB11 4JF
Tel: (01799) 522399
House open April to end September, Wednesdays to Sundays and Bank Holidays; park and gardens open at 10am

Berney Arms Windmill
Berney Arms
Norfolk NR31 0QA
Tel: (01493) 700605
Open daily April to end September

Castle Acre Priory
Castle Acre
Norfolk PE32 2XD
Tel: (01760) 755394

Castle Rising Castle
Castle Rising
Norfolk PE31 6AH
Tel: (01553) 631330

Denny Abbey
Cambridgeshire
CB5 9TQ
Tel: (01223) 860489
Open weekends only April to end of September

Framlingham Castle
Framlingham
Suffolk IP8 9BT
Tel: (01728) 724189

Grime's Graves
Lynford
Thetford
Norfolk IP26 5DE
Tel: (01842) 810656

Mistley Towers
Mistley, Essex
Key available from Mrs G Owens
Tel: (01206) 393884

Orford Castle
Orford
Suffolk IP12 2ND
Tel: (013944) 50472

Prior Hall's Barn
Widdington
Essex CB11 3ZB
Open weekends only April to end of September Tel: (01842) 750714 for further opening arrangements

Saxtead Green Windmill
Saxtead Green
Suffolk IP13 9QQ
Tel: (01728) 685789
Open April to end September, Mondays to Saturdays

Sibsey Trader Windmill
Sibsey
Boston
Lincolnshire PE22 0SY
Tel: (01246) 823349
Open on special milling days only

NATIONAL TRUST
East Anglia Regional Office
Blickling
Norwich
Norfolk NR11 6NF
Tel: (01263) 733471

East Midlands Regional Office
Clumber Park Stableyard
Worksop
Nottinghamshire S80 3BE
Tel: (01909) 486411

Anglesey Abbey & Garden
Lode
Cambridgeshire CB5 9EJ
Tel: (01223) 811200
House open April to mid-October, Wednesdays to Sundays & Bank Holiday Mondays; garden open April to end October, Wednesdays to Sundays & Bank Holiday Mondays (daily from early July to early September)

Belton House
Grantham
Lincolnshire NG32 2LS
Tel: (01476) 566116
Open April to end October, Wednesdays to Sundays & Bank Holiday Mondays (closed Good Fridays)

Blickling Hall, Garden & Park
Blickling
Norwich
Norfolk NR11 6NF
Tel: (01263) 733084
House open April to early November, Tuesdays, Wednesdays, Fridays to Sundays & Bank Holiday Mondays (closed Good Friday); garden open as house (also daily July & August); park daily all year

Felbrigg Hall, Garden & Park
Felbrigg
Norwich
Norfolk NR11 8PR
Tel: (01263) 837444
House & garden open April to early November, Mondays, Wednesdays, Thursdays, Saturdays and Sundays; park daily all year

Flatford: Bridge Cottage
Flatford
East Bergholt
Colchester
Suffolk CO7 6OL
Tel: (01206) 298260/298865
Open April to end October, Wednesdays to Sundays & Bank Holiday Mondays (also daily June to end September); (closed Good Fridays)

Horsey Windpump
Horsey
Great Yarmouth
Norfolk NR29 4EF
Tel: (01263) 733471 *(Regional office)*
Open daily April to end September

Houghton Mill
Houghton, near Huntingdon
Cambridgeshire PE17 2AZ
Tel: (01480) 301494
Open April to mid-October, Saturdays, Sundays and Bank Holiday Mondays (also end June to early September, Mondays to Wednesdays)

Ickworth House, Garden & Park
Ickworth
The Rotunda
Horringer
Bury St Edmunds
Suffolk IP29 5QE
Tel: (01284) 735270
House open April to early November, Tuesdays, Wednesdays, Fridays to Sundays & Bank Holiday Mondays; park & garden open daily all year (whole property closed Good Fridays)

Lavenham: The Guildhall of Corpus Christi
Market Place
Lavenham
Sudbury
Suffolk CO10 9QZ
Tel: 01787 247646
Open daily April to early November (closed Good Fridays)

Melford Hall
Long Melford
Sudbury
Suffolk CO10 9AH
Tel: (01787) 8808286
Open April to end October, Saturdays, Sundays & Bank Holiday Mondays (also Wednesdays & Thursdays, May to end September)

Oxburgh Hall, Garden & Estate
Oxborough
King's Lynn
Norfolk PE33 9PS
Tel: (01366) 328258
House & garden open April to early
November, Saturdays to Wednesdays

Paycocke's
West Street
Coggeshall
Colchester
Essex CO6 1NS
Tel: (01376) 561305
Open April to end October,
Tuesdays, Thursdays, Sundays &
Bank Holiday Mondays

Peckover House & Garden
North Brink
Wisbech
Cambridgeshire PE13 1JR
Tel: (01945) 583463
House open April to end October,
Weekends, Wednesdays and Bank
Holiday Mondays; garden open as
house (also Mondays and Tuesdays)

Wicken Fen
Lode Lane
Wicken
Ely
Cambridgeshire CB7 5XP
Tel: (01353) 720274
Open all year, except 25 December;
Fen Cottage open April to October,
Sundays & Bank Holiday Mondays

Wimpole Hall, Park & Garden
Arrington
Royston
Cambridgeshire SG8 0BW
Tel: (01223) 207257
Open April to early November,
Tuesdays to Thursdays, Saturdays,
Sundays & Bank Holiday Mondays
(also Fridays during August)

Woolsthorpe Manor
23 Newton Way
Woolsthorpe-by-Colsterworth
near Grantham
Lincolnshire NG33 5NR
Open April to end October,
Wednesdays to Sundays & Bank
Holiday Mondays (closed Good
Fridays)

MISCELLANEOUS
Bircham Windmill
Great Bircham
King's Lynn
Norfolk PE31 6SJ
Tel: (01485) 578393
Open daily April to end September
(Bakery & Tea Rooms closed
Saturdays)

Burghley House
Stamford
Lincolnshire PE9 3JY
Tel: (01780) 52451
House open daily from April to early
October (except on the Cross-Country
day of the Burghley Horse Trials);
gardens open as house and also week-
ends in late March

Cley Windmill
Cley-Next-the-Sea
Holt
Norfolk NR25 7NN
Tel: (01263) 740209
Open daily Whitsun to end
September

Colchester Castle
High Street
Colchester
Essex CO1 1YG
Tel: (01206) 282931
Open all year Mondays to Saturdays;
also Sundays March to end
November

Cromwell Museum
Grammar School Walk
Huntingdon
Cambridgeshire
Tel: (01480) 425830
Open daily (except Mondays and
Bank Holidays); open Good Fridays

Gainsborough's House
46 Gainsborough Street
Sudbury
Suffolk CO10 6EU
Tel: (01787) 372958
Open daily all year (except non-Bank
Holiday Mondays, Good Fridays &
25 December to 1 January)

Holkham Hall
Wells-Next-the-Sea
Norfolk NR23 1AB
Tel: (01328) 710227
Open daily from end May to end
September (except Fridays &
Saturdays); also open Easter & Bank
Holidays

Layer Marney Tower
near Colchester
Essex CO5 9US
Tel: (01206) 330784
Open daily April to end September
(except Saturdays)

Little Hall
Market Place
Lavenham
Suffolk CO10 9QZ
Tel: (01787) 247179
Open Easter to end October,
Wednesdays, Thursdays, Saturdays,
Sundays & Bank Holiday Mondays

Lowestoft Maritime Museum
Sparrow's Nest Park
Whapload Road
Lowestoft
Suffolk NR32 1XG
Tel: (01502) 561963
Open daily May to end October

Moot Hall & Museum
Aldeburgh
Suffolk
Open May, weekends; daily June to
end September

Norfolk Lavender Ltd.
Caley Mill
Heacham
Norfolk PE31 7JE
Tel: (01485) 570384
Open daily all year (except
Christmas break)

St Osyth Priory
St Osyth
Essex CO16 8MZ
Tel: (01255) 820492
House open May to end September
(except Saturdays) & Easter week-
ends; garden open daily

Sandringham
Estate Office
Sandringham
Norfolk PE35 6EN
Tel: (01553) 772675
Open Easter to mid-July and early
August to October

Wingfield Old College
Wingfield
near Eye
Suffolk IP21 5RA
Tel: (01379) 384505
Open Easter to end September,
Saturdays, Sundays & Bank Holiday
Mondays

Woodbridge Tide Mill
Tide Mill Way
Woodbridge
Suffolk
Tel: (01473) 626618 (Warden's
office)
Open Easter & daily May to end
September; October weekends only

BIBLIOGRAPHY

Bacon, Jean & Stuart, *The Suffolk Shoreline*, Segment, Colchester, 1984

Batcock, Neil, *The Ruined and Disused Churches of Norfolk (*East Anglian Archaeology Report No 51*)*, Norfolk Archaeological Unit, Dereham, 1991

Beardall, CH, & Co., *The Suffolk Estuaries*, Segment, Colchester, 1991

Beckett, RB, *John Constable's Correspondence: the Family at East Bergholt 1807-1837*, Suffolk Records Society, Ipswich, 1962

Beckett, RB, (comp.), *John Constable's Discourses*, Suffolk Records Society, Ipswich, 1970

Bellamy, David, & Quayle, Brendan, *Wetlands: An Exploration of the Lost Wilderness of East Anglia*, Sidgwick & Jackson, London, 1990

Betterton, Alec, & Dymond, David, *Lavenham: Industrial Town*, Dalton, Lavenham, 1989

Blake, PW, Bull, J, & Co, *The Norfolk We Live In*, Jarrold, Norwich, 1958 (rev 1964)

Bond, Arthur, *The Walsingham Story Through 900 Years*, Guild Shop, Walsingham, 1960

Chainey, Graham, *In Celebration of King's College Chapel*, Pevensey Press, 1987

Chambers, J, *A General History of the County of Norfolk* (2 Vols), John Stacy, London, 1829

Clarke, R Rainbird, *East Anglia*, Thames & Hudson, London, 1960

Clarke, WG, *In Breckland Wilds* (2nd ed rev by R Rainbird Clarke), Heffer, Cambridge, 1937

Cobbett, William, *Rural Rides* (2 Vols), Dent, London, 1912

Cook, Olive, *Breckland*, Hale, London, 1956

Cox, J Charles, *Essex* (Little Guides series), Methuen, London, 1909

Darby, HC, *The Draining of the Fens*, Cambridge University Press, Cambridge, 1956

Defoe, Daniel, *A Tour Thro' the Whole Island of Great Britain* (2 Vols), Davies, London, 1927

Dutt, William A, *Suffolk* (Little Guides series), Methuen, London, 1904

Dymond, David, *The Norfolk Landscape*, Alastair Press, Bury St Edmunds, 1990

Edgson, Vivien Mary, *A Study of Mersea Island to 1970*, Wren, Colchester, 1993

Edwards, Russell, *The River Stour*, Dalton, Lavenham, 1982

Edwards, Russell, *The Suffolk Coast*, Dalton, Lavenham, 1991

Ewans, Martin, *The Battle for the Broads*, Dalton, Lavenham, 1992

Fendall, Caroline (sel) *A Norfolk Anthology*, Boydell Press, Ipswich, 1972

Gadney, Reg, *Constable and His World*, Thames & Hudson, London, 1976

George, Martin, *The Land Use, Ecology and Conservation of Broadland*, Packard, Chichester, 1992

Glyde, John, *The Norfolk Garland*, Jarrold, London, 1872

Greenway, Diana, & Sayers, Jane (trans), *Jocelin of Brakelond: Chronicle of the Abbey of Bury St Edmunds*, OUP, Oxford, 1989

Haigh, David, *The Religious Houses of Cambridgeshire*, Cambridgeshire County Council, Cambridge, 1988

Haining, Peter, *Maria Marten: The Murder in the Red Barn*, Castell, London, 1992

Harrod, Wilhelmine, *Norfolk: a Shell Guide*, Faber, London, 1958

James, MR, *Suffolk and Norfolk*, Dent, London, 1930

Jebb, Miles, *Suffolk*, Pimlico, London, 1995

Jones, Clarence, *The Life and Works of Constable*, Parragon, 1994

Long, Neville, *Lights of East Anglia*, Dalton, Lavenham, 1983

Mason, HJ, & McClelland, *Background to Breckland*, Providence Press, Ely, 1994

Mason, HJ, & McClelland, *An Introduction to the Black Fens*, Providence Press, Ely. 1973

Mee, Arthur, *Cambridgeshire (*King's England series*)*, Hodder & Stoughton, London, 1937 (rev 1965)

Mee, Arthur, *Essex (*King's England series*)*, Hodder & Stoughton, London, 1940 (rev 1966)

Mee, Arthur, *Norfolk (*King's England series*)*, Hodder & Stoughton, London, 1940

Mee, Arthur, *Suffolk (*King's England series*)*, Hodder & Stoughton, London, 1941 (rev 1949)

Morris, Christopher, (ed), *The Journeys of Celia Fiennes*, Cresset, London, 1947

Mottram, RH, *Norfolk* (Vision of England series), Elek, London 1948

Orna, Bernard & Elizabeth, *Flint In Norfolk Building*, Running Angel, Norwich, 1984

Pevsner, Nikolaus, *Bedfordshire & the County of Huntingdon and Peterborough* (Buildings of England series), Penguin Books, Harmondsworth, 1968

Pevsner, Nikolaus, *Cambridgeshire* (Buildings of England series), Penguin Books, Harmondsworth, 1954

Pevsner, Nikolaus, *Essex* (Buildings of England series), Penguin Books, Harmondsworth, 1954

Pevsner, Nikolaus, and Harris, John, *Lincolnshire* (Buildings of England series), Penguin Books, Harmondsworth, 1964

Pevsner, Nikolaus, *North-East Norfolk & Norwich* (Buildings of England series), Penguin Books, Harmondsworth, 1962

Pevsner, Nikolaus, *North-West and South Norfolk* (Buildings of England series), Penguin Books, Harmondsworth, 1962

Pevsner, Nikolaus, *Suffolk* (Buildings of England series), Penguin Books, Harmondsworth, 1961

Price, Harry, *The End of Borley Rectory*, Harrap, London, 1946

Rackham, Oliver, *The Last Forest: The Story of Hatfield* Forest, Dent, London, 1989

Ravensdale, Jack, & Muir, Richard, *East Anglian Landscapes*, Michael Joseph, London, 1984

Reynolds, MJ (ed) *About Suffolk: A Suffolk Anthology*, Boydell Press, Ipswich, 1958

Sandon, Eric, *Suffolk Houses: A Study of Domestic Architecture*, Antique Collectors' Club, Woodbridge, 1984 (1st pub 1977)

Scarfe, Norman (ed), *A Frenchman's Year in Suffolk, 1784*, Boydell Press, Woodbridge, 1988

Scarfe, Norman, *Cambridgeshire: A Shell Guide*, Faber, London, 1983

Scarfe, Norman, *Essex: A Shell Guide*, Faber, London, 1968

Scarfe, Norman (trans), *Innocent Espionage: The La Rochefoucauld Brothers' Tour of England in 1785*, Boydell Press, Woodbridge, 1995

Scarfe, Norman, *Suffolk: A Shell Guide*, Faber, London, 1960

Scarfe, Norman, *The Suffolk Landscape*, Alastair Press, Bury St Edmunds, 1987

Smart, Alastair, & Brooks, Attfield, *Constable and his Country*, Elek, London, 1976

Stanley, Louis T, *Cambridge: City of Dreams*, Allen, London, 1987

Weston, Chris & Sarah, *Claimed by the Sea*, Wood Green, Norwich, 1994

INDEX